CLARENDON ARISTOTLE SERIES

General Editors

J. L. ACKRILL AND LINDSAY JUDSON

ARISTOTLE
POLITICS

BOOKS III AND IV

*Translated
with Introduction and comments
by*

RICHARD ROBINSON

*With a Supplementary Essay
by*

DAVID KEYT

CLARENDON PRESS · OXFORD
1995

Oxford University Press, Walton Street, Oxford OX2 6DP

Oxford New York
Athens Auckland Bangkok Bombay
Calcutta Cape Town Dar es Salaam Delhi
Florence Hong Kong Istanbul Karachi
Kuala Lumpur Madras Madrid Melbourne
Mexico City Nairobi Paris Singapore
Taipei Tokyo Toronto
and associated companies in
Berlin Ibadan

Oxford is a trade mark of Oxford University Press

Published in the United States
by Oxford University Press Inc., New York

© Richard Robinson 1962
Supplementary Essay and Select Bibliography © David Keyt 1995

First published 1962
Reprinted with new material 1995

British Library Cataloguing in Publication Data
Data available

Library of Congress Cataloging in Publication Data
Data available
ISBN 0-19-823591-7
ISBN 0-19-823592-5 (Pbk.)

Printed in Great Britain
on acid-free paper by
St. Edmundsbury Press
Bury St Edmunds, Suffolk

CONTENTS

INTRODUCTION

1. *The preparation of this book*

J. L. Austin, a few years before his early death, conceived and proposed to the Clarendon Press the idea of new translations of portions of the writings of Aristotle, adapted to the interests of contemporary philosophers. From long works like the *Politics* only parts were to be taken, in order to keep the volumes small; but these parts were not to be less than complete books, in the sense of 'book' appropriate to ancient Greek writings.

Austin invited me to do something from the *Politics*. I agreed; and we decided on Books III and IV. We spent a long morning together in the late autumn of 1959, going over the first third of my translation of Book III. His beautiful intelligence and reasonableness, with his kind encouragement, made it a very profitable and happy morning. His illness and death then cut off any further collaboration.

I have received much help from Sir David Ross, the greatest interpreter of Aristotle to the English, particularly with regard to the new readings in his edition of the text of the *Politics*. For it is Sir David's new text that I have translated here: '*Aristotelis Politica* recognovit brevique adnotatione critica instruxit W. D. Ross, Oxonii, e Typographeo Clarendoniano, MCMLVII.' I have paragraphed much more often than he does, and I have inserted some index numbers; but I have tried to translate precisely his text in every line except 1294ª28 and 1300ª39. Disagreements between myself and previous translators, while in some places due to differing opinions about the meaning of the Greek, are in other places due to a novelty in Sir David's text.

Mr. P. A. Brunt of Oriel College has kindly read and criticized the whole of the translation of Book III. Mr. J. L. Ackrill of Brasenose College, appointed editor of the series in succession to Austin, has kindly done the same for Book IV. These scholars have caused me to make many changes; but I have persisted in some renderings of which they disapprove.

I thank Oriel College for giving me the sabbatic leave during which I did most of this work. I thank the Institute for Advanced Study for receiving me during that leave and giving me ideal conditions of work. And I thank Professors Harold Cherniss and H. T. Wade-Gery for very kind encouragement and help during my stay at the Institute.

2. *Defects of the* Politics

Aristotle's *Politics* is a book with great defects, which probably lose it many readers. The style is often awkward and often obscure, usually owing to excessive brevity, sometimes owing to excessive tentativeness or caution. The order of thought is annoyingly inconsequential. Aristotle announces a programme and then does not follow it, or follows it very imperfectly. Tiresome repetitions occur and the same subject is treated again: Aristotle divides democracy into species three times in the *Politics*, and twice in the books translated here.

Much of the writing is very tentative, either in manner or in meaning or both. 'Perhaps' is one of Aristotle's favourite words; and his way of saying that something is false is prone to be: 'But perhaps this is not wholly correct' ($1282^{a}14$). Sometimes he merely reports other people's views and refuses to judge for himself. He disappoints us by not taking a stand on what we consider essential political principles. (Hence the summaries which I have prefixed to the chapters sometimes make him seem more explicit than he is, and sometimes suggest a greater confidence about what he concludes than I really feel.) It is useless to go to him for political dogma and certainty.

When he does take a stand, it is liable to seem inconsistent with something he says elsewhere. Newman wrote that 'a plentiful crop of [unreconciled contradictions] usually comes to light whenever we make a careful study of Aristotle's teaching on any subject' (I 284).

The fact is, probably, that the *Politics* is a collection of long essays and brief jottings pretending to be a treatise. It is thoughts written at different times by a man whose thoughts were abundant and always developing, in intervals between much business and much study of other kinds. It makes a far less unified impression than most of his works except the *Metaphysics*.

Aristotle no doubt loses some readers also by his scholasticism. He is the great master of logical distinctions, and he loves to divide classes into smaller classes. It is true that he keeps his logical interest down in his *Politics*; but a faint flavour of it remains, and may be as repellent to most of those interested in politics as garlic is to a northern palate.

Finally, Aristotle loses readers because his egalitarianism is much narrower than ours. The number of those whom he can imagine as becoming his political equals never includes even half the adult male population, much less the whole human race. 'Only a few people within the state can ever be happy and . . . the structure of the state is determined by the ethical needs of a very small number of the population' (George Boas, *Amer. J. of Philology*, 1943, p. 191).

3. *The aporetic method*

The *Politics* becomes less irritating after one has realized and accepted the aporetic method which it often uses.

Aristotle is not writing out elementary principles of politics to be learned by docile and ignorant beginners. He is discussing difficulties felt by those who have already reflected on political matters. His word for such a difficulty or problem is 'aporia'. After indicating an aporia, he recites the considerations that have made it an aporia, including arguments both for and against a certain solution. These arguments may or may not have true premisses, and their premisses may or may not be strong grounds for their conclusion. Aristotle by no means personally recommends all the premisses and inferences to which he draws your attention. He merely lays them before you as things to be considered in making up your mind. He believes it worth your while to know the arguments that have been given, or might be given, for and against a certain view. He does not write for those who only want dogmatic conclusions, which they can then adopt on the authority of Aristotle. Usually he does give his own conclusion; but sometimes he gives it in such a tentative form (for instance, as a question) that it is easy not to recognize it. In his aporetic discussions we are liable to mistake the beginning for his own view when it is not, and to mistake the end for a question when it is his own conclusion!

Aporetic procedure is different from demonstration as in Euclid, where we first state definitions and axioms and then prove theorems from them. Aristotle recommends demonstration in his *Analytics*, and may have influenced the form of Euclid's geometry by doing so. His own writings, however, do not practise demonstration so much as they practise aporetic. The differences are that aporetic has no abiding set of axioms and definitions but only a succession of *ad hoc* premisses, that the reader is not required to accept these premisses, that there are several arguments for each conclusion instead of only one, that these arguments are usually not proofs but merely probable, and that there are arguments on both sides of a theorem.

Aristotle never examined his own aporetic as thoroughly as he examined the geometers' demonstration, and he does not give the following justification of aporetic in political science. Demonstrated certainty is attainable in mathematics; but it is unattainable about matters of fact and questions of action. Political science deals with matters of fact (as 'Do democracies last longer than oligarchies?') and questions of action (as 'Shall we have juries?'). Any demonstration of an answer to such questions as these, proceeding from a single set of axioms, would be an untrustworthy guide in practice. It would be folly or worse to rely solely on these axioms and consider nothing else. Practice requires judgement, not demonstration; and practical judgement demands that we do not narrow our thoughts to a single set of axioms, but widen them to take in the great mass of facts, valuations, wishes, fears, opinions, and principles, that are relevant to an important action. We must collect as much of this great mass as we can, weigh each consideration, and then—judge! The judgement is always a leap in a way that a mathematical conclusion is not a leap. But it is the best thing to do in the circumstances; and certainly we all make more correct judgements than correct proofs, because we judge far more often than we prove.

Judgement is inferior to demonstration in the following respect, among others. The demonstrator can give his whole reason, but the judge cannot. The demonstrator can give his whole reason because it is nothing but one derivation from one set of premises. The judge cannot give his whole reason because it is nothing less than the whole of our interests and principles and circumstances. He is placed in a false position when asked what was the reason for his decision. Hence we ought to listen to the undemonstrated statements of the old and wise and experienced no less than to proofs, as Aristotle says elsewhere (*Nic. Eth.* 1143ᵇ12). But this tempts the old to pronounce from passion and without prudence. Hence the old ought to give as far as possible that reason for their decisions which can never be given completely. The aporetic method is an attempt to do this.

4. *Value of the* Politics

In spite of its defects, the *Politics* is the greatest work there is in political philosophy, and very well worth study.

Even the style of the book has its value. While its obscurity and disconnexion make it distasteful to some people, others are delighted by its brevity, its sincerity, its absolute rejection of rhetoric, its reasonableness towards the reader, and its extreme economy in the use of loftiness and passion.

The *Politics* consciously aims at being of practical use, and it is so. It puts behind itself (in the parts here translated) the disastrous urge of the political aesthete or revolutionary 'to grasp this sorry Scheme of Things entire, . . . shatter it to bits—and then remould it nearer to the Heart's Desire'. Instead of that, the *Politics* takes up the prosaic, necessary work of maintaining our precarious polity in a going and tolerable condition.

It is practical for us as well as for its contemporaries, although their States were cities and ours are nations. The difference in size makes all the difference between representative and direct democracy; but it makes no difference with regard to political selfconsciousness. Aristotle wrote for people who were politically selfconscious and inquisitive, who no longer took the rule of a traditional monarch as both right and inevitable, but regarded the political structure as something to be made and remade by man for man; and such are we too. Pascal's idea that Aristotle wrote politics for kings and emperors is wholly false of the *Politics*; this work is not addressed to his imperial pupil Alexander, but to burghers and lawgivers of Athens and the other Greek cities. (Pascal XIII 250 Brunschvicg.) The curious view that Book VII 1–12 of the *Politics* is really Aristotle's *Alexander or On Colonies*, and addressed to Alexander, is certainly false. (Endre von Ivánka, *Die aristotelische Politik* usw., 1938.)

'But so many political ideas have arisen since Aristotle, and his ideas are so obvious now.' It is true that very strikingly different political ideas have arisen since Aristotle wrote the *Politics*, especially those of Marx. It is plausible also that Aristotle's political ideas have a certain obviousness now. But then, if his ideas are obvious, those of Marx must be wrong, and it must be important that the ancient truths should be reasserted.

The truths of politics, and of Aristotle's *Politics*, are old; but they are not really obvious. They have been said before today, and they tend to bore us when we are looking for intellectual novelty rather than for political peace and justice. But they are obvious only to those who are both experienced and prudent and cannot be seduced by the desire for novelty or by pity for men's miseries. They were invisible to many fashionable intellectuals in the third and fourth decades of this century.

There is an admirable calmness and impartiality about the *Politics*. Aristotle is far from being partisan, and far from holding that all who disagree with him are wicked. He does not scream 'immoral and dishonest!' at those who are to the right or left of himself. If there is any fault in his political emotion, it is not priggery but excessive detachment. I suppose he never had a vote at Athens, and was never a full member of a great and typical city-state. He observed the Athenian democracy like de Tocqueville observing that of the United States, in the country but not of it, without a personal ambition or a party to push, actuated by intellectual interest and benevolence. His attitude to cities was not that of a preacher but that of a biologist and physician. He did not want to tell them what they morally ought to do, but how they were constructed and how they could live in peace and contentment.

The *Politics* is sane and judicious and cautious and prudent. Hignett judges it immeasurably superior in breadth of treatment and soundness of judgement to the *Constitution of Athens*, another political work attributed to Aristotle by most students but denied to him by Hignett. Sound judgement in politics cannot be evolved in the head, like mathematics, but requires historical knowledge of political experience. Genuine historical knowledge is hard to come by, as Thucydides taught the world (I 20–22). It requires criticism and examination and labour. It does not come to those who accept tradition as they hear it and aim at interest rather than truth. Aristotle upon the whole has learned Thucydides' lesson. We know that he took great and methodical pains to acquire wide and accurate knowledge of the constitutional histories of the cities. His political conclusions are clearly based on this knowledge; and, of course, he had many more States to observe than we have, because his States were small (as Sinclair remarks, pp. 5–6).

There are times, however, when Aristotle's empiricism fails him in politics. Sometimes he resorts to the purely logical classifications and divisions which he loved. Sometimes he makes the almost universal mistake of inventing man's prehistory out of his head: the first book of the

Politics, not translated here, opens with a perfectly imaginary account of the origin of cities. And when he says we 'see' that so and so is the case, this seeing is liable to be mental intuition, not physical sight. It is easy to think he is being empirical when he is not.

5. *The subject of the* Politics

The subject of Aristotle's *Politics* is not exactly politics as we understand the word. Rather it is constitutions. That is why Book III begins with the words: 'In the study of constitutions, and of the nature and character of each constitution'.

His conception of a constitution is not quite the same as ours. It seems much the same when he writes that 'a constitution is an ordering of the city in respect of its offices and particularly of the sovereign one' (1278ᵇ8). For we easily think of this 'ordering' as consisting in a set of laws, written or unwritten, governing the appointment of the officers and their duties. But Aristotle does not think of the constitution as merely a set of fundamental laws, or even as primarily such; and his book is not about laws (cf. 1286ᵃ3).

His conception of a constitution is almost more sociological than political. Primarily a constitution is to him a way of political life, a set of habits of political action and valuation, and the laws involved in it are only expressions or safeguards of this way of life. This was probably the usual Greek way of looking at it; for it is found in Plato and Thucydides too. The four constitutions which Plato describes in *Republic* VIII are social moods rather than legal systems. Similarly, although Thucydides makes Pericles represent his Funeral Speech as a description of the Athenian constitution (II 37, 1), the Speech contains little about law and much about habits of action and valuation.

Thucydides' Pericles finds it natural to speak of 'practice and constitution and manners' as if all three were the same kind of thing (II 36, 4).

There is another difference between Aristotle's conception of a constitution and ours. Our constitution is something relatively abstract. We reach it by abstracting, from the whole spectacle of a society, a small aspect consisting of the more fundamental rules by which the members of that society proceed in politics. Aristotle, on the contrary, usually thinks of the constitution concretely, as being the members themselves, the men who are united as being the politically active members of that society. A constitution tends to be laws to us, but men to him. We with a little exaggeration can say that 'the constitution is all the rules that govern the government'. But when Aristotle exaggerates it comes out much more concretely: he simply says that 'the constitution is the government' (1278^{b}11).

'The constitution' and 'the political community' are equivalent phrases in his language. In the first two books of the *Politics* he refers to his topic as being 'the political community' (I 1252^{a}7 and II 1260^{b}27). In the next two books, those translated here, he refers to his topic as being the 'constitution' or 'constitutionality' (III 1274^{b}32 and IV 1293^{b}30). This is not a change of plan.

Aristotle's constitution is the constitution of some city. The Greek city was an independent sovereign State, conducting its own foreign affairs; it was not a municipality, like our cities, subject to correction from above and having no say in foreign policy. The Greeks therefore needed and had no separate word for 'State'. This is well known and makes little difference. We only have to remember that what Aristotle says about his cities is relevant to our States, not to our cities.

Aristotle does not use the word 'constitution' or 'polity' in the sense of citizenship or franchise, as Thucydides often did. That is one ambiguity which he mercifully avoids. He has, however, another and much more deceptive ambiguity; for he sometimes uses the word 'constitution' to mean one specific form of constitution. This ambiguity begins to appear in III 7 and is commented on there.

6. *Aristotle on the end of the city*

Aristotle often speaks of nature as if she were a person and perhaps a divine person. Nature is a kind of goddess to him, not explicitly acknowledged as such but acting as such. He considers himself able to tell us of certain universal principles on which nature acts. For instance, he tells us in *Politics* I 2 that 'Nature never makes things penuriously, like smiths making a Delphic dagger. She makes one tool for one purpose, because each tool is best when it serves one purpose only' ($1252^{b}1-5$).

The most important of Aristotle's principles about nature is that 'Nature makes nothing idly or without purpose' (*Politics* $1256^{b}21$, and in other works). The phrase is often translated 'Nature does nothing in vain'; but that is not the meaning. Aristotle is not denying that nature has her failures; he is denying that she is ever aimless. She may fail to produce what she intends; but she always intends to produce something. This is his first physical postulate.

He also holds, which is not quite the same proposition, that every natural thing has a purpose. In an organic part like the tongue, the part has as its purpose some contribution to the existence of the whole. But Aristotle believes the principle of all natural wholes also. In them, however, the purpose is immanent, not transcendent; it is to realize something in themselves. All natural things are given an aim by nature; and this aim is the most real feature of the thing, the feature that makes it what it is, in fact, the 'nature' of it.

Now the city is a natural thing, according to Aristotle, although he contemplates the possibility that there was someone who first put it together (1253^{a}30). That the city is natural is implied by his famous phrase, 'man is by nature a political animal'; and he offers argument for it in the first book of the *Politics*. The argument proceeds partly by means of an imaginary history of the origin of cities, partly by recalling the inadequacy of groups smaller than a city and asserting that a city is 'completely selfsufficient, practically speaking', and lastly by saying that nature, who makes nothing without a purpose, has given man the ideas of good and bad and right and wrong, sharing in which makes a household and a city (1253^{a}7–18).

From the two doctrines, that every natural thing has a purpose, and the city is a natural thing, it follows syllogistically that the city has a purpose. Aristotle has a firm hold of this conclusion. The city has a natural aim.

It is important to realize the logical nature of Aristotle's doctrine that the city has an aim.

We can sometimes empirically ascertain what the makers of a constitution intended to achieve by it; Jefferson, for instance, may have left statements of what he meant the constitution of the United States to produce. We can sometimes empirically ascertain what the citizens think they are achieving by their constitution or some part of it; Gallup, for instance, could find out by questioning a sample what people think is the purpose of some clause in the United States constitution. Quite apart from what anybody thinks, we can sometimes see in history that a certain State has regularly aimed at a certain result, even if none of its citizens ever acknowledged such an aim. Thus perhaps we can see in history that Russia has always

aimed at the imperial control of her neighbours, and that
Japan until the end of the nineteenth century aimed at
complete isolation from her neighbours.

But this is not what Aristotle means. He is not giving us
an empirical or historical report about *some* cities. He is
offering us a universal affirmative statement about *all*
cities. He means that *every* State *always* has a purpose, and
it is *the same* purpose for all States at all times. That is what
he deduces from his principles that the State is a natural
thing and every natural thing has a purpose.

But it seems perfectly clear that this is false. States do not
all have one and the same purpose all the time, except
possibly the purpose of maintaining their own authority
over their own citizens. Perhaps we cannot find a State
that did not care whether its subjects obeyed it or not, just
because as soon as it ceased to care about this it would
cease to exist. But I doubt whether we can find any further
purpose that has been common to all States. Even the purpose of maintaining law and order and decency among the
citizens, while very frequent, is perhaps not universal.

Aristotle realized this well enough. He did not mean to
claim that all States actually have had one and the same
purpose always. He himself said that in few or no States
except Sparta does the lawgiver seem to have cared about
upbringing and behaviour (*Nic. Eth.* 1180ª25).

The explanation is that Aristotle's doctrine that every
city has one and the same end is imperative rather than
descriptive. He means that every city *ought* to have one
and the same end. Statements about the end of a thing are
often concealed imperatives, ways of announcing a decision and imposing it on others, and Aristotle's statement
about the end of the city is of this kind. It is not like 'we
have observed that Russia is always trying to conquer her
neighbours'. Rather it is like 'States ought to make their

citizens good men, and the citizens ought to submit to this'.

If we take Aristotle's statements about nature as being strictly physical and descriptive, and not carrying any implied imperative, then some imperative premiss needs to be added to them in order to reach his conclusion. This might be that we ought so far as we can to fulfil the purposes of nature, at least in those instances which concern ourselves. Since we are men, we ought to fulfil the purpose or work which nature assigns to her creature man. And, since we are citizens, we ought to fulfil the purpose which nature assigns to her creature the city. Without this practical premiss we cannot logically get to Aristotle's practical conclusion, if we take his statements about nature as purely descriptive. Commands do not follow from mere descriptions of nature. There must be a command concealed somewhere in the premisses, such as 'Do what nature does!' or 'Help nature to fulfil her purposes!'

What then is this aim of the city, this one identical aim that every city has by nature? Since the city is the supreme community, the good at which it aims is the supreme good (1252^{a}1–6). The supreme good is the good life. While the city arises for the sake of life, it exists for the sake of good life (1252^{b}30). 'The end of a city is the good life' (1280^{b}39).

And what is the good life? It is good actions, not companionship (1281^{a}2–4). It involves the goods of both circumstance and body and soul, but those of circumstance and body to a moderate amount, and those of the soul, including courage and temperance and justice and wisdom, to an extreme (1323^{a}26–^{b}3). A man has so much of happiness as he has of goodness and wisdom and action in accordance therewith (1323^{b}21–22). Fundamentally the good life is the life of virtuous action.

It follows that the purpose of the city, given to it by

nature, is to make and keep the citizens virtuous men doing virtuous deeds. This is what every city always *ought* to aim at, though it rarely does; and this is what we as citizens ought to see that our city does. We ought in our political activities to aim at making the citizens virtuous. 'Lawgivers make the citizens good by training them; to do this is the wish of every lawgiver; those who do not do it well are in error; herein differs a good constitution from a bad one' (*Nic. Eth.* 1103^b3–6). Since 'living temperately and patiently is not pleasant to the many, particularly to the young, upbringing and education should be laid down by laws, which will not be painful when they have become habitual. Perhaps it is not enough for the citizens to enjoy right care and upbringing while young. Since they ought to practise these habits when grown up too, we should need laws for these matters also, and indeed for the whole of life generally' (*Nic. Eth.* X 9, 1179^b33 ff.).

Aristotle's train of thought begins with an account of nature and ends with a recommendation or command. Starting with the proposition that nature makes nothing without a purpose, he ends with a command to lawgivers to organize the city so that it makes the citizens virtuous, and an implicit command to the citizens to submit themselves to such lawgivers. Such inferences, where the premiss is a statement about nature and the conclusion is a command, have become and remain very common, which is part of Aristotle's enormous effect upon us.

This is the paternalistic doctrine of the State, that the State is related to its citizens in the same natural way as a father to his children, and ought to make and keep its citizens virtuous as a father ought to make and keep his children virtuous. It has been immensely influential in subsequent history. It has always been and still is the conscious and explicit doctrine of the Roman Catholic Church;

and it also works unconsciously but powerfully in a great many non-Catholic minds.

7. *Critique of Aristotle's paternalism*

This paternalism is the most fundamental and most grave error in Aristotle's politics.

In the first place, his initial premisses about nature are never properly ascertained. He was a great student of nature, and gave us in his zoological works much information about her. But these doctrines that nature makes nothing without a purpose, and that every natural thing has a purpose, are not the fruit of his zoological work. They are hypotheses imposed on nature contrary to appearances. They are recommended to Aristotle by his intuitive feelings as to how nature *must* be, not by his observations as to how she *is*.

As to his premiss that the city is a natural thing, the city looks much more like an artificial thing, if we oppose nature to art as Aristotle often does, and if we admit as he does that cities are sometimes deliberately made by lawgivers. The name 'nature', when used to cover a product of art in this way, loses definiteness and moves towards being a general name for anything there is. In modern terms we can say that most cities are products neither of nature nor of art, but of that third power, culture. Certainly the city is not made likely to be a natural thing by the weak arguments Aristotle brings for this, such as his armchair history of the origin of cities.

For his practical conclusion Aristotle requires, though he does not state it, the premiss that it is our duty to fulfil the purposes of nature. This duty is void for uncertainty, to use a legal phrase; for it is uncertain, not to say unascertainable, what the purposes of nature are. But it would be void even if we all agreed as to what the purposes of nature are; for we are not required to fulfil any purposes nature may have. We are entitled to fulfil our own purposes, and to make any use of nature that we please in doing so. And so we constantly do. For instance, when adult humans drink cows' milk, that is clearly a diversion of nature's purpose to ours, unless you can believe with Aristotle that nature made all huntable or tameable animals for the benefit of man (1256^{b}16–22).

Aristotle himself would have come to disbelieve this premiss if he had stated it explicitly. It is a premiss which convinces only while concealed. It lay concealed for Aristotle in his statements about the ends or purposes of nature. Once we have explicitly asked ourselves why we should do anything just because nature does it, or why we should aid nature in her purposes, we see that there is no reason why we should. Let nature look to her own purposes, if she has any. *We* will look to *ours*.

Aristotle cannot have a right to prescribe to all cities what they shall aim at. The policy of a State is a matter for the decision and choice of the citizens. It is not the prerogative of theorists or of officers not responsible to the citizens. Politics and policies are fundamentally decisions, preferences, and choices. Aristotle is too highhanded in thinking himself and other 'accurate observers' (1280^{b}28) entitled to prescribe our policies for us. At the most he may say negatively what the aim of the city morally may not be, and exclude those aims that are immoral, such as the conquest of other cities and the selfish domination of a group of citizens over the rest. On the positive side he may only express his preferences, not issue commands.

The enterprise of attempting to make other adults virtuous is to be rejected, when it goes beyond the minimum of protecting ourselves against assault and murder and fraud and theft. That assault and murder and fraud and theft must be minimized is clear; and this is enough to justify us in removing by legal force the freedom of others to do these things. In other words, we may try to make men act with common decency. But we may not try to make men live 'the good life', meaning by this some more exacting standard of behaviour than common decency. We have no right to demand more from our fellows than common decency. Making or changing the characters of other men is a highly dubious enterprise, to be attempted only when the character to be changed is generally agreed to be very harmful to others and the prospect of success is considerable.

One of the reasons, why we have no right to demand more than common decency from our fellow citizens, is that it is by no means certain what the good life is, or whether there is only one kind of good life; while, on the other hand, it is quite certain that many good kinds of life have been ignored or even disapproved by many who have talked about the good life. Aristotle, for instance, has not the faintest idea that the life of making and enjoying works of art is a very good life, or that the life of the explorer is a very good life.

The State has less right than the individual has to try to make individuals live a higher life, because States are less virtuous and less intelligent than individuals. The State inevitably acts through changing and conflicting officers, which gives its action much incoherence and stupidity. The endless, disheartening stupidity of States can be read in history. Also the State inevitably executes its policies through a multitude of petty functionaries who have no conception of a higher life. The stupidity of States in moral matters is clear to see in most censorships and most prosecutions for immorality. Thucydides shows both the stupidity and the wickedness of ancient Athens.

States are as incompetent to teach us human goodness as are lions and pigs.

All States that have existed for more than fifty years are in fact moral criminals. That is to say, their past acts include moral crimes which they have not expiated or repented of. Every one of the new States that have been liberally created since 1918 will soon be a criminal too. Such beings have no call to undertake a moral education of adults.

Aristotle's main political principle is therefore bad. If everything else in the *Politics* depended on that, the *Politics* would be a bad book. Fortunately it does not. Aristotle often envisages other and more acceptable ends for the State, when he is not explicitly asking himself what the end of the State is. In one place he says that the good constitutions are those which aim at the common advantage, as opposed to the private advantage of the governors. This is far better. We shall often disagree as to what is to our common advantage, but that is better than having it decided that our common advantage is to be educated by the State into the State's ideal of manhood.

These two accounts of the purpose of the State, that it is to make the citizens virtuous and that it is the common advantage, could be brought into some relation by saying that one of the virtues is the disposition to seek the common advantage. But publicspiritedness has not yet been recommended as a major virtue and is not one of the virtues that Aristotle recognized. The nearest virtue to it which he recognized was the munificence of the rich man who directed and paid for public services. Plato came closer to the idea; but he also came closer to the frequent and harmful habit of confusing the common advantage of the citizens with a supposed advantage of the State distinct from any common advantage of the citizens. Publicspiritedness, or the pursuit of the general good which upon the whole helps each individual, has been much confused with patriotism, or the pursuit of the particular good of the State as an individual person, which may be glory or conquest and may hinder rather than advance the general good of the citizens. But they are distinct; and, whereas public-spiritedness is a virtue, patriotism is a vice. If they are ever generally distinguished, and national pride generally repudiated in favour of publicspiritedness, the harm done by States will greatly decrease.

In another place Aristotle's remarks tend to suggest that it is an end of the State to get justice done, though he is thinking only of one small part of justice, namely justice in the distribution of political power. It certainly is an end of the State to get justice done. The reign of some approximation to justice is the best justification there can be for a State's existence, and a perfectly proper goal for it to aim at.

But most of the goodness in Aristotle's *Politics* occurs in the course of talk about means, not ends. The proper ends of a State are whatever ends, among those that are morally legitimate, its citizens wish it to aim at, and especially justice, security, common decency, and useful enterprises like roads. The trouble is that the means to these ends, that is the State itself, is inevitably also a likely cause of great evils. Hence it is an important question of politics how to have a State which will procure the obvious aims of a State without also causing a great deal of misery and evil. A State is a kind of person, a monster person created by individual persons for their advantage, but tending like Frankenstein's monster to ruin its creators. One great question of politics is therefore a question of means, how to organize the State, our means to certain necessary ends, so that it achieves those ends without at the same time causing great evil. And it is means that Aristotle is really discussing most of the time in the part of the *Politics* here translated. The different kinds of constitution that he envisages are the different kinds of means that we may choose to secure our common ends.

8. *The translation*

My aim has been to produce a writing which will make upon twentieth-century readers as nearly as possible the same impression as Aristotle's text made or would have made upon his contemporaries. Only such a writing constitutes a translation proper, as opposed to a paraphrase or explanation or commentary, or to a variation on the theme. The ideal translation would make exactly the same impression on its readers as the original made on the original readers, both in thought and in feeling and in emotion.

The ideal translation is impossible. No two sentences in different languages can ever make wholly the same impression. Still less can they do so if the two languages are two thousand years apart. Thus the translator is condemned never to achieve his aim, and always to produce an imperfect and unsatisfactory result. He always gives a worse account of his author than even a thirdrate actor can, because the actor can utter the very words that the author wrote.

From the inevitable imperfection of translation it follows that a rendering should never be rejected on the mere ground that it is imperfect, but only on the ground that there is another possible rendering which is less imperfect. The undoubted fact that 'city' is not equivalent to 'polis' is not a good reason for rejecting the former as a translation of the latter; the question is whether any other English expression is less objectionable for this purpose.

Probably nearly all translators admit the general principle that a translation should make as nearly as possible the same impression as the original. Yet there is one important respect in which most translators cannot bear to apply this principle, namely where they think their author's style is bad. If a sentence seems to them obscure or ugly or ungrammatical, they avoid reproducing the defect in their translation. Sometimes they justify this to themselves by thinking that the defect was tolerated in ancient Greece but is intolerable now, or that the importance of spreading Aristotle's thoughts abroad excuses alterations of his style. More often, probably, they merely feel that they want their revered author to make a good impression.

I desire to follow the principle even in these awkward cases. I want to reproduce Aristotle's style as nearly as possible, including those aspects of it which may seem bad to me or my readers. Only so can I come as near as may be to fulfilling the promise which I implicitly make to my readers in calling this a translation. It may also happen that something which displeases me in Aristotle's style will, nevertheless, unexpectedly, please some of my readers. And I ought to confess that it is easier for me than for most translators to bring myself to try to reproduce Aristotle's queer style, because unlike most people I really enjoy it.

A translation should not be less obscure than its original. Aristotle's style is often so dense, tightlipped, and sketchy, that it takes some rereading before you see what his train of thought was, although his words are mostly common words and his sentences mostly short. It undoubtedly made this impression on ancient Greeks as much as it does on us. It is not, and it never was, flowing, loose, hackneyed, or 'newspaper' Greek. Therefore nothing written in English of that sort is a proper translation of it. This is my apology for giving you a book that requires slow reading and considering.

There are, of course, occasions when Aristotle by exception seems to display the opposite defects, either by writing a sentence that is too long and complicated, or by labouring the obvious. These too I have tried to reproduce as they are.

A translation should not be less ugly than its original. We should resist the temptation to try to write better than our author did. I have therefore tried to keep Aristotle's disconcerting changes of tense and number, the unnecessary length and complexity of occasional sentences, and the anticlimax at the end of some of them.

At the same time, I do not admit the common opinion that Aristotle's style is generally ugly, or that he has none. His style is beautiful. Many persons fail to perceive its beauty; but there is nothing unusual in failing to perceive some particular kind of beauty. The beauty of Aristotle's style depends largely on his conceptual power; but it is genuine aesthetic beauty for all that, and as sensuous as verbal beauty ever is.

A translation should not be less simple or naïve than its original. Aristotle wrote in a way that a twentieth-century reader easily feels to be surprisingly naïve for a 'professor' of 'philosophy' or of 'social science'. Modern English gives immense opportunities for sophistication and imposingness. Modern political English in particular is very often pompous and dishonest, as George Orwell makes clear in his essay on 'Politics and the English Language' in the volume called *Shooting an Elephant, and Other Essays*. A translator should resist the fear that a true rendering will cause some readers to dismiss Aristotle as simpleminded. I have tried not to substitute sophistication for his simplicity, or faded metaphors for his directness, or to give a synonym when he repeats the same word.

A translation should not be less ambiguous or elusive or

vague or general than its original. The translator should resist the temptation to tell his readers it was a robin when his author only says it was a bird. He may put in more words if they are necessary to make the English as specific as the Greek; but he may not put in more words in order to make the English more specific than the Greek, even if the Greek seems to us intolerably ambiguous. Mr. Warrington in his Everyman translation has been led by this temptation into the howler of making Aristotle suppose that Cleisthenes did his work after the Thirty Tyrants (1275ᵇ36; Everyman translation, p. 69).

More generally, we may say that a translator should not introduce into his version an Aristotelian doctrine which he knows to lie behind what the text says. If he wants to tell the reader what lies behind, he should add a note, or write a commentary.

A translation is a shameful form of book in this respect, that the translator implies statements which he does not know to be true. For he offers a translation of every sentence in his original, and he thereby implies that he knows that this is what the original sentence means. But sometimes he does not know what it means, and is only guessing as well as he can. The translator of Aristotle is often in this position.

I always composed a version of each of Aristotle's sentences before looking at the version of any other translator. After writing my own version I compared it with others. Whenever I judged anything in another version to be better than mine, I adopted it. Resemblances between other versions and that which I now publish are therefore sometimes due to my having copied the other version. Sometimes, however, they are accidental. I believe that no translator or publisher will object to my borrowings. The common aim of all of us is to produce the best version possible.

TRANSLATION AND COMMENT

III 1–5. THE CITIZEN

III 1. SUMMARY. *The citizen is whoever has a right to take part in deliberative and judicial office in a city.*

TRANSLATION. 1274ᵇ32. In the study of constitutions, and of the nature and character of each constitution, almost the first thing to ask is just what is a city. For people dispute whether a certain act was an act of the city, or not of the city but of the oligarchy or of the tyrant. And we see that the politician and the legislator are entirely concerned with the city, while the constitution is a certain ordering of those inhabiting the city.

1274ᵇ38. But since the city is a composite, like any other whole consisting of many parts, it is clear that one must first look for the citizen. For the city is a certain number of citizens. We must examine, therefore, who should be called a citizen and who the citizen is. This too is often disputed. People do not all agree as to who is a citizen; for a certain kind of person who is a citizen in a democracy is often not a citizen in an oligarchy.

1275ᵃ5. We must put aside those who acquire the title of citizen in some other way, for instance by decree. The citizen is not a citizen through residing somewhere, since foreigners and slaves are also residents. Nor is a man a citizen because he shares in the rights of a citizen so far as to sue and be sued, since a commercial treaty may confer that right. In many places, moreover, the resident foreigners do not enjoy even these rights completely, but must have a patron, so that their part in this kind of association is somewhat imperfect. Similarly, minors who by reason of youth have not yet been enrolled, and old men

who have been exempted, must not be called quite simply
'citizens', but rather citizens 'of a kind', with addition of
the words 'not yet full' or 'superannuated' or the like—it
does not matter what, since what is being said is plain.
Similar difficulties can be raised and solved about exiled
and disfranchised persons. But we are looking for the
citizen proper, who is free from every such charge calling
for correction.

1275ᵃ22. The citizen proper is distinguished by nothing
else so much as by having a share in giving judgement and
exercising office. Some offices are limited in point of time,
so that either they can be held only once, or they can be
held again only after some definite period. But there is
also an office without limitation, namely that of the judge
and the assemblyman. Perhaps someone would say that
such persons are not officers at all, and do not share in
office on this account. Yet it is ridiculous to deny that
persons in a position of the highest authority are officers.
But let this pass; it is a question of name. There is no name
for what is common to a judge and an assemblyman,
which applies to both of them. To distinguish it let us call
it 'office without limitation'. We take a citizen to be one
who shares in this.

1275ᵃ33. Such, roughly, is the definition that would best
fit all those who are called citizens. But we must not forget
that, when a subject-matter includes things differing in
kind, of which one comes first and another second and so
on, there is either nothing or hardly anything common to
all these things as such. Now we see that the constitutions
differ in kind among themselves, and that some are posterior and others prior, since the mistaken and perverted
ones must be posterior to those which are not mistaken.
(What we mean by 'perverted' will be clear later.) Hence

the citizen must differ in different constitutions. The citizen we have defined is primarily a citizen in a democracy. He may or may not be so in another constitution. In some there is no demos, and they do not have an assembly but convocations, and law cases are judged in separate courts. Thus in Sparta cases of contract are judged by one or other of the Overseers, cases of homicide by the Elders, and others perhaps by other officers. So too at Carthage all cases are tried by certain officers.

1275ᵇ13. But our definition of the citizen can be saved, as follows. In the other constitutions it is not the unlimited officer who is assemblyman and judge but the limited, since to all or some of the latter is assigned deliberation and judgement on all or some questions. These considerations make plain who is the citizen: we say that whoever has a right to take part in deliberative and judicial office is a citizen of that city. And a city is, to put it simply, a number of such persons large enough for selfsufficiency of life.

III 2. SUMMARY. *In practice the citizen is defined as one whose parents were both citizens.*

TRANSLATION. 1275ᵇ22. In practice a citizen is defined as one whose parents were both citizens, not merely his father or his mother. Some wish to go even farther back, for example, two or three or more generations. But, some ask, how, on this coarse political definition, will that third- or fourth-generation ancestor be a citizen? Gorgias of Leontini said, perhaps half in perplexity and half in jest, that, as mortars were what the mortarmakers made, so Lariseans were what the Craftsmen made, since some of them were Lariseanmakers.[1] But it is simple: if they had

[1] Double pun. The word for 'craftsman' was also the word for a kind

a part in the constitution by the given definition they were citizens. In any case the definition of a citizen as one whose father or mother was a citizen cannot be applied to the first inhabitants or founders.

1275ᵇ34. More difficult, perhaps, is the case of those who obtained a share in the constitution through a revolution, as when at Athens after the expulsion of the tyrants Cleisthenes enrolled many resident foreigners and slaves in a tribe. The dispute here is not who is a citizen, but whether he is wrongly or rightly a citizen. One might, however, go further and argue that one who is wrongly a citizen is not a citizen, on the ground that wrong means the same as false. But since we see that some persons hold office wrongly, so that we shall say of them that they *are* in office but not rightly so, and since the citizen is defined by reference to some office (the citizen is he who shares in such and such an office, as we said), it is plain that we must say that even these persons are citizens.

COMMENT (III 1–2). Aristotle is not thinking of citizens as opposed to aliens, or of the two streams into which passengers are divided on landing: 'British subjects this way; aliens that way.' When he says that 'a certain kind of person who is a citizen in a democracy is often not a citizen in an oligarchy', he does not mean that this kind of person is an alien in an oligarchy. He is not asking in what sense a woman is called a citizen although she has no political rights, though he himself uses the word in this sense when he writes that 'in practice a citizen is defined as one whose parents were both *citizens*'. He does not anywhere in his *Politics* examine anything like being a trueborn native Englishwoman, and hence an unquestionable member of the State of England no matter how small her political rights.

On the contrary, Aristotle is thinking of certain political privileges and duties which never belonged to all trueborn Athenians, because they never belonged to any Athenian woman. His question is about certain privileges and duties that belong, or ought to belong, to some

of officer in some city-states; and the word 'Larisean' meant either a citizen of Larisa or a kind of large pot made at Larisa.

but not all of the trueborn Athenians. It is the question which of the citizens in the large sense (including women) are or ought to be also citizens in some narrow sense.

'Citizen' in this narrow sense is an ascriptive word. To call a person a citizen is to ascribe to him certain political privileges and duties. Hence two different but connected questions arise: What are these privileges and duties; and to whom should they belong? The meaning of 'citizen' is not simple, but has these two sides. Aristotle does not quite see that he is answering the first question in his first chapter and the second question in his second chapter. He supposes that he is answering the same question in both chapters, but in a more practical and less refined way in the second chapter. Yet he almost suggests the true relation when he writes: 'We must examine, therefore, who should be called a citizen and who the citizen is.'

The question may be taken historically, as the question what actually used to be the practice or is now the practice in some historical State: to whom do contemporary Athenians in fact assign what duties and privileges? Or it may be taken as a question of choice: to whom shall we, or ought we to, assign what duties and privileges? To take it as a question of choice is fundamental, for the historical interpretation is the question what somebody else has chosen. This is the explanation of the fact, remarked by Aristotle, that 'the citizen must differ in different constitutions'. Democracies and oligarchies choose to assign certain privileges and duties to different sets of people.

The declaration, that a citizen (in the narrow sense) is anyone whose parents were both citizens (in the broad sense), means that we assign these duties and privileges to anyone whose parents we recognize as being both citizens in the broad sense. The fact that we could not apply this to the first generation is irrelevant, because we do not have to deal with the first generation. We have to deal only with the generation now growing up.

The privilege chosen by Aristotle as constitutive of citizenship is having a right to take part in deliberative and judicial office. That is as if we were to give the title of 'citizen' only to those few Englishmen who have both the right to vote in the House of Commons and the right to vote guilty or not guilty on a bench of magistrates. But those who have this combination of rights in England are a very much smaller proportion of the people on English soil than those who had them in Aristotle's Athens were of those on Attic soil. The theory there was that the adult male free citizen population itself conducted all government and justice. And the size of the city allowed this to be fairly near the truth.

III 3. SUMMARY. *A city is a society of citizens sharing a constitution. When the constitution changes, it is no longer the same city.*

TRANSLATION. 1276ª6. Whether they are rightly citizens or not connects with the dispute mentioned earlier. Some people are in doubt what to count as an act of the city. For example, when an oligarchy or a tyranny changes into a democracy, some people wish not to fulfil contracts, on the ground that it was not the city but the tyrant who received the consideration; and they wish to do many other things of the sort, because they believe that some constitutions are maintained by force and not for the common good. However, since some democracies also are maintained in this way, the acts of a constitution of this sort and of an oligarchy and of a tyranny must equally be declared acts of the city.

1276ª17. There seems to be a close relation between this difficulty and the question when we ought to say that the city is the same and when not the same but another one. To seek an answer to this by reference to the place and the persons is very superficial; for the place and the persons can be parted, and some of them can occupy one place and others another. This must be pronounced a fairly simple problem, for the ambiguity of the word 'city' leaves plenty of room to manœuvre.

1276ª24. Also simple is the question when men inhabiting the same place are to be held to constitute one city. Certainly not when they are enclosed in the same *walls*; for the Peloponnese could be surrounded by a single wall. Babylon is perhaps actually like that, and every city whose extent is more that of a nation than a city, since they say that two days after it was captured part of the city did not yet know it.

1276ᵃ30. It will be useful to examine this question at another time, since the politician ought to know how big a city should be, and whether it should contain more than one nation. But when we have the same men inhabiting the same place, are we to say that it is the same city as long as the inhabitants are of the same stock, although some are always dying and others being born, just as we commonly call rivers and springs the same although the stream is always coming and going? Or should we say that this makes the men the same but the city different? Since the city is a society, and a society of citizens sharing a constitution, it would seem that, when the constitution takes another form and differs, the city also cannot be the same. Just so we call it a different chorus if it is now comic and now tragic, although often the men are the same. And similarly we call every other society and compound different, if the form of the compound is different. Thus we say it is a different scale of the same notes, if it is now Dorian and now Phrygian. This being so, it is clear that a city is to be called the same mostly by looking to the constitution. It can be given a different or the same name whether the inhabitants are the same or entirely different.

1276ᵇ13. Whether it is right to fulfil or not fulfil contracts when the constitution of the city changes is another matter.

COMMENT. 'When we ought to say that the city is the same and when not the same but another one.' We certainly *do* say it is the same city after a change of constitution; we do not say that Athens became another city each time the democracy was overthrown or restored, nor did the ancient Greeks. Aristotle appears to be criticizing our usage and saying that we are not talking as we ought to talk. This is a rare thing for him to do; ordinarily he piously accepts actual usage.

It is also in this case a mistake, because our usage here is perfectly proper. Everything is both the same and different, according to the criteria employed. It is not every 'taking another form and differing' that determines the end of one particular and the beginning of another. For instance, a person's ceasing to be a child is not the end of that person. The constitution is not the criterion by which we call a city or a State one and the same. If it were, the absurd consequence would follow that a city could not change its constitution without committing suicide. Aristotle, instead of criticizing our usage, should have inquired what is its criterion.

He concludes that every change of constitution involves the end of one city and the beginning of another. This doctrine appears nowhere else in the *Politics*, and seems quite inharmonious with the rest of the work, though perhaps not logically inconsistent. It is particularly discordant with the emphasis in Book I on the city's being a natural growth.

He tantalizes us by raising but dismissing the important practical question whether obligations incurred by the city before a revolution should be discharged by the city thereafter. He never discusses the moral obligations of cities, or whether they have moral obligations, or whether they are moral agents or persons.

III 4. SUMMARY. *The goodness of a citizen cannot be identical with the goodness of a man, for several reasons, notably because the goodness of a citizen varies with the constitution, while the goodness of the good man is always the same. Only the good ruler will be both a good citizen and a good man.*

TRANSLATION. 1276^{b}16. Connected with these matters is the following question: are we to say that the goodness of a good man and a good citizen are the same, or not? If this ought to be examined, we must first get some outline of the goodness of the citizen. We say, then, that the citizen, like the sailor, is one of the partners in a society. Sailors are unlike each other in capacity: one is an oarsman, another a helmsman, another a bowman, and others have other such names; but it is clear that, while the most precise account of each one's goodness will be peculiar to himself, there will also be some common account fitting them all alike. The safety of the voyage is the business of them all, for each of the sailors aims at that. Similarly the citizens, though unlike each other, have the safety of the society as their business; and their society is the constitution. Hence the goodness of the citizen must be relative to the constitution; and, since there are several kinds of constitution, there clearly cannot be one single goodness of the good citizen, namely perfect goodness. But the good man, we say, has one single goodness, namely perfect goodness. Plainly, therefore, it is possible to be a good citizen and yet not possess the goodness of a good man.

1276^{b}35. One can go into the same argument by raising the question in another way, namely with regard to the best constitution. For, if it is impossible for a city to consist entirely of good men, it is nevertheless necessary that each should do his own job well, and do it out of goodness; but, since it is impossible for the citizens to be all alike, there would not be one single goodness of a citizen and a good man. This is because the goodness of the good citizen must belong to them all (only so can the city be the best), whereas the goodness of the good man cannot do so, since the citizens in the good city cannot all be good men.

1277^{a}5. Moreover, the city consists of unlike members. As an animal consists of soul and body, and a soul of reason and desire, and a household of man and woman, and a proprietorship of master and slave, so a city consists of all these and of other unlike forms in addition. Necessarily, therefore, the goodness of all the citizens is no more identical than is that of the leader and the sideman in a chorus.

1277^{a}12. That it is not always the same is plain from these considerations. But will there be anyone in whom the goodness of a citizen and the goodness of a man do coincide? We say that the good ruler is also a good and wise man, but that the citizen need not be wise. Some say that the very upbringing of a ruler is different. The sons of kings appear to be brought up on the arts of riding and war. And Euripides says:

> No subtleties for me . . .,
> But what a city needs . . .,

implying that a ruler has a special upbringing. If then the goodness of a good ruler is identical with that of a good man, while the subject also is a citizen, the goodness of a man would be identical with that of a certain citizen but not with that of every citizen. The goodness of a ruler and of a citizen are not the same. Perhaps this is why Jason said he was hungry when not a tyrant: he did not know how to be a private man.

1277ᵃ25. Furthermore, we praise the power to rule and to obey, and it seems that the goodness of an approved citizen consists in being able both to rule and to obey well. If therefore we make the goodness of the man to consist in ruling, but that of the citizen in both, the two would not be equally praiseworthy. Since then there are occasions when they seem different, and ruler and subject should not learn the same things, while the citizen should know and share in both, the consequence becomes clear.

1277ᵃ33. There is such a thing as master rule, namely rule concerning those necessities which the ruler need not know how to make, but rather to use. The former is in fact servile. (By the former I mean to be able actually to provide menial activities.) We speak of several kinds of slave, because there are several kinds of work. One kind of work is that of the manual labourers. These are, as the very name itself implies, those who live by their hands. They include the working craftsman, which is why in ancient times the workmen were not eligible for office in some places, until the extreme demos arose. The functions of subjects of this sort are not to be learned by the good politician or by the good citizen, except that he himself may perform them on occasion to benefit himself, since that is not a case of master and slave.

1277^{b}7. But there is a kind of rule which rules over free men of the same stock. This is what we hold political rule to be. The ruler must learn it by being ruled, squadron-leading by being led, generalship by being generalled, colonelcy and captaincy likewise. Hence it is also a good saying that only those who have been ruled can rule well. While good ruling is distinct from good obeying, the good citizen must possess the knowledge and the ability both to obey and to rule; and the goodness of a citizen consists in understanding the government of free men in both directions. Both of them belong to the good man, even if the temperance and justice of a ruler are different.

1277^{b}18. It is also plain that even the goodness of the free subject, for example his justice, will not be always the same, but will take different forms according as he is ruling or being ruled. Similarly, the temperance and courage of a man are different from those of a woman. A man would seem cowardly if he were no braver than a brave woman; and a woman would seem talkative if she were no more decorous than the good man. The household management of a man is also distinct from that of a woman, his business being to get and hers to keep.

1277^{b}25. The only goodness peculiar to a ruler is his wisdom. The others, it seems, are necessarily common to rulers and subjects; but the subject has true opinion instead of wisdom. The subject is like a flutemaker, and the ruler is like the flautist who uses the flute.

1277ᵇ30. The above makes clear whether or not the goodness of a man is the same as the goodness of a citizen, and in what respect they are the same and in what respect different.

COMMENT. Aristotle's difficulty here appears to be different from any of ours. We often worry whether the State's orders conflict with our conscience, or whether our duty to the State conflicts with our duty to our family, or whether a politician can be an honest man. None of these questions occurs to Aristotle.

Aristotle's difficulty arises from the following beliefs which he holds. (1) There is such a thing as the perfect goodness of a man, and it is one and only one. Every perfectly good man, if there were any, would be exactly like every other perfectly good man in respect of his goodness.

(2) Aristotle, like every one else, had vaguely in mind a list of the qualities or virtues that would constitute the perfectly good man, including courage, temperance, wisdom, and justice. But, like his contemporaries and unlike us, he tended to include in this list masculinity and nobility. His word for 'courage' was the same as his word for 'manliness'; and he felt that the perfection of human character would have to include a certain masculine masterfulness. He also felt that not to display the leisure and freedom of the upper class was inevitably to be less than a perfect man.

(3) Yet, like everybody else, he distinguished, thirdly, between a good and a bad woman, and a good and a bad servant, and a good and a bad citizen, and desired to have the former and not the latter in each case.

This combination of valuations makes the difficulty that he wrestles with here, in a chapter more aporetic even than usual in the *Politics*. The good woman and the good servant are only slightly noticed here. Aristotle gives his attention to the good citizen. It seems that the goodness of the good citizen will be various, not single, both because there are many different jobs to be done in a city and because different kinds of constitution ask for different kinds of citizen. This conflicts with the singleness of perfect human goodness. And it seems clear that an outstanding and frequently manifested part of the goodness of the good citizen will be obedience to laws and orders, which unfortunately conflicts with Aristotle's feeling that the perfect man is a giver of orders, not a recipient of them. Aristotle is thus driven to the view, extraordinary and gloomy to us, that 'the citizens in the good city cannot all be good men'.

We westerners of the twentieth century often feel conscientious shock and horror when we meet this side of Aristotle's valuations. But let us beware of insincerity. Vast numbers of us cannot help feeling profound admiration for the really masterful man, Napoleon or Stalin, no matter how immense the misery he causes.

This is not to deny that Aristotle's conception of the ideal man needs correction. It is to suggest that nearly everybody's conception of the ideal man needs correction.

The most important alteration, probably, is to reject the belief that ideal human goodness is of one and only one kind. In other words, to remove the word 'the' from the expressions '*the* ideal man' and '*the* perfect human goodness'. It is better to say that we can only very dimly see, as yet, what best or better forms human goodness might take, and how many of them there might be.

Different people have different ideas as to what qualities make a good man. This often has an effect on translators. The translator, realizing that Aristotle's conception of a good man is different from ours, is inclined to react by saying that Aristotle's word 'good' does not mean good, and must be given some other translation, perhaps 'gentlemanly'. This is a mistake. Aristotle's *agathos* means good and should be translated as such. His *arete* means goodness and should be translated as such. (He had no noun *agathia*, though he had *andragathia* and *kalokagathia*, both of which mean the goodness of a man.)

It is odd that the philosophic tutor of Alexander the Great should write that 'the sons of kings appear to be brought up on the arts of riding and war'.

III 5. SUMMARY. *Workmen and labourers are citizens in some constitutions but not in others.*

TRANSLATION. 1277^b33. One problem concerning the citizen remains: Is it really the case that the citizen is he who has the right to take part in the government, or should we call workmen also citizens?

1277^b35. If we are to include these persons also, who

have no part in governing, such goodness cannot belong to every citizen, this man being a citizen. But, if such a person is not a citizen, in what class are we to put him? He is not a resident foreigner, nor a stranger.

1277^{b}39. Can we not say that there is no absurdity here? He is in the same position as slaves and freedmen. It is certain that we must not call citizens all those without whom there would be no city. Even children are not citizens in the same way as adults. Adults are citizens simply; but children are only hypothetically so. They are citizens, but imperfect ones.

1278^{a}6. In ancient times the working class was slave or foreign in some places, which is why most of them are so today; and the best city will not make a workman a citizen. If, however, he too is a citizen, then we must say that the goodness we spoke of does not belong to every citizen, nor to every free man, but only to those who are released from necessary services. Those who provide necessary services for one man are slaves. Those who do it for the community are workmen and labourers.

1278^{a}13. A brief examination of this will make plain how things stand with these people; in fact, it is clear from what we have said. Since there are several constitutions, there must also be several kinds of citizen and especially of subject citizen. Consequently, the workman and the labourer must be citizens in some constitution and cannot be so in others. For example, they could not be so in what is called an aristocratic constitution, that is, where honours are given according to a man's goodness and merit, since it is impossible to practise goodness while living the life of a workman or labourer. In oligarchies a labourer cannot be a citizen, because eligibility for office depends on high assessments; but a workman can be, for in fact the majority of craftsmen are rich. At Thebes there was a law that no one could hold office unless he had been ten years out of trade. In many constitutions the law even brings in some foreigners. Thus in some democracies a man is a citizen if his mother was a citizen. In many places the same applies to bastards. However, since it is lack of genuine citizens that makes them create such citizens as these (underpopulation is the cause of these laws), when they have plenty of people they gradually reject first those who have a slave parent, then those whose father is not a citizen, and finally they make citizens only those whose parents are both townsmen.

1278ª34. It is clear, then, that there are several kinds of citizen, but the citizen most properly so called is he who has a right to honours, as Homer in fact implied when he wrote: 'as if I were some dishonoured immigrant'. The man who has no right to honours is like a resident foreigner. Where this kind of thing is done secretly, that is in order to deceive one's fellow inhabitants.

1278ª40. Whether or not we should say that the goodness of the good man is the same as that of the good citizen is clear from what has been said: he is the same in some cities and not in others; and where he is the same he is not every citizen there, but the politician who is in control of public affairs, or capable of being in control of them, either alone or in concert with others.

COMMENT. This chapter exhibits Aristotle's feeling that it is an essential part of human goodness to live the life of leisure. He infers that workmen and labourers cannot be good men. He does not feel any reluctance or shame or sorrow in accepting this conclusion. We, on the contrary, are liable to be so intensely ashamed as to pretend we do not believe it if we do. Perhaps, if it were not for this intense shame, we should think that it is almost impossible to be a high type of man while passing one's working life on an assembly-line.

In deciding whether a workman is a citizen Aristotle uses a definition of the citizen that is, verbally at least, different from that he reached in III 1. He now says that 'the citizen most properly so called is he who has a right to honours'. 'Honours' seems to suggest a more definite and honourable office than merely being an assemblyman or a juror, which was enough to make a man a citizen in III 1.

III 6–8. THE CONSTITUTIONS

III 6. SUMMARY. *Man is by nature a political animal, coming together in cities for the sake of the good life. The constitution of a city is the ordering of its offices, and particularly of the sovereign one. If the constitution aims at the common good it is correct, since the city is a society of the free. But, if it aims at the good of the rulers only, it is despotic and perverted.*

TRANSLATION. 1278ᵇ6. That having been determined, we come to the question whether to distinguish more than one kind of constitution, and, if so, how many, what they are, and what the differences between them are.

1278ᵇ8. A constitution is an ordering of a city in respect of its offices and particularly of the sovereign one. For in every city the government is sovereign, and the constitution is the government. Thus in democracies the demos is sovereign, in oligarchies on the contrary the few, and we say that these are different constitutions. The same reasoning will apply to the others.

1278ᵇ15. First we must lay down (1) the purpose of a city, and (2) how many kinds of rule there are concerning man and social life.

1278ᵇ17. (1) In our first discussions, where we examined household management and mastership, we also said that by nature man is a political animal. Because of this, mankind, even when they need no help from each other, none the less seek companionship. At the same time their common interest brings them together, in so far as there falls to each of them some part of the good life. This, then, is the chief end, both of each individual and of them all in common. They do, however, also come together and maintain political society just for the sake of keeping alive. For there is perhaps some element of the good even in mere living itself, so long as it is not too overburdened with the difficulties of existence. It is evident that most men endure much hardship in their struggle for life, as if it had a kind of prosperity in itself and were naturally sweet.

1278ᵇ30. (2) The accepted kinds of rule can easily be distinguished. In fact we often do so in our popular works. The rule of a master, although in truth the advantage of the natural slave is identical with that of the natural master, is nevertheless rule for the sake of the master, and only incidentally benefits the slave because the mastership cannot be preserved if the slave perishes. Rule over children and wife and the whole household, which we call household management, is for the sake either of those ruled or of something common to both sides. Essentially it is for the sake of the ruled, as we see the other arts to be, such as medicine and athletic coaching; but accidentally it could also benefit the rulers, since there is nothing to prevent the coach from being sometimes himself one of the athletes, just as the navigator is always one of the sailors.

1279ᵃ4. The coach or navigator seeks the good of those he directs; but when he is himself one of these he incidentally shares in the benefit; for then he is, in the latter case, a sailor, and, in the former, he becomes one of the athletes while remaining their coach. In the same way in politics, when there is equality and similarity of the citizens, each expects to have his turn at office. Formerly, in the proper manner, they expected to bear the burden of office in turn, and then being released to pursue their private good, as in office they had been pursuing the other man's interest. But now, because of the emoluments of office and public affairs, they want to be in office continuously, as if being in office kept the sickly in perpetual health; for in that case also they would probably pursue office.

1279ª17. It is clear that those constitutions which seek the common advantage are correct and accord with simple right, while those which seek only the advantage of the rulers are all mistaken and perversions of the correct constitutions. For the latter are all masterships, whereas the city is a society of the free.

COMMENT. When Aristotle says that the difference between a correct and a perverted constitution is that the one 'seeks' the common advantage and the other the advantage of the ruler, it makes a difference whether we take 'constitution' abstractly or concretely.

Abstractly interpreted, his thought would be that the abstract constitutional arrangement is such that, no matter what the intentions of the rulers may be, the result tends to the common advantage, or that the abstract constitutional arrangement has the effect of making the rulers aim at the common advantage. This political idea has been prominent since the eighteenth or seventeenth century; but it is never unmistakably expressed in Aristotle. He comes nearest to it when he writes that 'each officer decides well if he has been trained by the law' (1287ᵇ25).

Concretely interpreted, Aristotle means that a set of persons politically organized as a sovereign city are a correct constitution when their rulers do in fact aim at the common advantage, and a perverted constitution when their rulers do in fact aim at their private advantage, so that a constitution might change from correct to perverted simply by the rulers' changing their intention, without there being anything that we should call a 'constitutional' change.

One would expect that Aristotle's subsequent discussion of the various constitutions he recognizes would settle the question what he means here, and show whether the difference between monarchy and tyranny, and that between aristocracy and oligarchy, and that between 'constitution' and democracy, lie in some difference of their laws and legal arrangements, or in the difference of their rulers' intention. Yet I do not find this to be clearly so.

This division of constitutions into those which do, and those which do not, aim at the common advantage, replaces Plato's division of them in his *Statesman* into those which do, and those which do not, proceed according to law. Whether a constitution is likely to secure the common advantage is probably the most important question about it; and probably Aristotle is here bringing this question into greater prominence than Plato ever did. On the other hand, he asks whether a constitution 'seeks' the common advantage, which is not quite the same question. The important question about rulers and constitutions is what they actually produce rather than what they seek to produce. Furthermore, acting according to law is a great means of securing the common advantage. Again, whether rulers are acting according to law can be determined much more objectively than what they are seeking. Later in the *Politics* Aristotle tends to revert to Plato's criterion, in effect though not explicitly.

Another possible way of dividing constitutions is according to whether or not the subjects consent to the rule of the rulers. Aristotle does not use this as a general principle for dividing constitutions, although he sometimes implies that it makes the difference between kingship and tyranny (e.g. 1313ª15). Division by reference to the consent of the subjects will not always give the same classes as division by reference to the intention of the rulers.

In dividing constitutions Aristotle makes no use, here or elsewhere, of Plato's distinction between constitutions where the rulers know, and those where they do not know, what is really good and right. It is not practical politics, as we see when we imagine ourselves appointing an officer to decide who knows and who does not know about the politically good and right.

III 7. SUMMARY. *The sovereign must be one or few or the many. When the sovereign rules for the common advantage, we have the three correct constitutions: kingship, aristocracy, and the so called 'constitution'. Their perversions, aiming at the advantage of the ruler, are tyranny, oligarchy, and democracy.*

TRANSLATION. 1279ª22. The next business is to examine the number and nature of the constitutions. And first the correct constitutions; for when they have been distinguished the perversions will be clear too.

1279ª25. Since constitution and government mean the same, and a government is the sovereign in a city, and the sovereign must be either one or few or the many, when the one or the few or the many rule for the common advantage these are necessarily correct constitutions; but they are perversions when they rule for the private advantage either of the one or of the few or of the majority. For those who do not participate either should not be called citizens or ought to share in the benefit.

1279ª32. The customary name for a monarchy that looks to the common advantage is 'kingship'. For a rule of more than one but only a few it is 'aristocracy', either from the rulers' being the best men or from its aiming at the best for the city and its participants. When the majority governs for the common advantage, this is called by the common name of all the constitutions, a 'constitution'. A natural usage; for, whereas one man or a few can stand out in goodness, it is hardly possible for a number of men to be perfect in every goodness. Only military excellence can be found in a majority. Hence in this constitution the most sovereign part is the fighting part, and those who share in it are those who possess arms.

1279ᵇ4. The perversions of the above are as follows. Tyranny is the perversion of kingship, oligarchy of aristocracy, and democracy of 'constitution'. Tyranny is a monarchy aiming at the advantage of the monarch. Oligarchy aims at that of the prosperous, democracy at the advantage of the needy, none of them at the common profit.

COMMENT. We have here a new sense of 'constitution', the specific sense in which 'constitution' is one of the six species of constitution in the generic sense. This is what may be called a 'genus–species' ambiguity, where the same word is used to mean now a genus and now one of the species of that genus. There are other examples of it in Aristotle's thought.

English scholars often use the word 'polity' for this specific sense, thus removing the ambiguity. This is sometimes a good thing to do in discussing Aristotle; but it is a bad thing to do in translating him, because a translation is inaccurate if it is less ambiguous than the original. It is particularly bad when there is considerable doubt in the Greek which sense Aristotle intends (as in 1297ᵃ6, 8, 12, 14).

There is some mystery about this specific 'constitution', although the chapter gives a formal definition of it as the constitution where the many are sovereign and rule for the common advantage. The chapter itself seems to imply another definition when it says that 'those who share in it are those who possess arms' (1279ᵇ3). These two definitions are not obviously equivalent. This uncertainty about what he means continues through the later chapters where he deals with 'constitution' at length. Another mystery is whether he is thinking of some actual constitution or of some ideal. He has statements implying that 'constitutions' have occurred from time to time; but he also has the statement that 'the middle constitution' has never or rarely occurred (1296ᵃ37), where 'the middle constitution' appears to be polity. Perhaps the solution is that, while constitutions called polities had often occurred, Aristotle was changing the meaning of 'polity' to something that had not often or ever occurred.

The division into the one and the few and the many has two great defects. (1) Which one? Which few? Which many? If the citizens number a thousand, then a thousand different ones can be selected from them, and far more than a thousand different fews, and far more than a thousand different manies. For example, even so small a group as ten persons contains 386 distinct manies or majorities. If Aristotle meant *any* majority or *any* few or *any* one, he should not have used the word 'the'. In fact, however, after introducing them as 'one or few or *the* many', he refers to them as '*the* one or *the* few or *the* many', as if he meant some particular many, not any of the many manies that could be selected out of the whole.

(2) Why does he not say 'one or few or many *or all*'? Surely that all should rule is a fourth possibility in the same division. It is difficult to believe either that he thought the rule of all impossible, or that he thought it identical with the rule of a many.

This implies two possible senses of the word 'democracy', namely the rule of all and the rule of some majority. These correspond to the western and eastern senses of 'democracy' today. Westerners call their States democracies because, they claim, all rule in them; but easterners call theirs democracies because, they claim, in them the proletariat, which is a majority, rules. Did Aristotle mean by 'democracy' the rule of all or, rather, the 'dictatorship of the proletariat'? The question cannot be confidently answered by considering Aristotle's word 'demos'. 'Demos' is an undefined word with him. Sometimes it is a synonym for 'democracy', as in 1294ª11. Sometimes it means whoever is the sovereign in a democracy, but leaves us to guess who that is. But note that at the end of III 7 he says that 'democracy [aims] at the advantage of the needy'.

III 8. SUMMARY. *Yet the real difference between oligarchy and democracy is that the former is the rule of the prosperous and the latter is the rule of the needy. It is accidental that the prosperous are few and the needy many.*

TRANSLATION. 1279ᵇ11. We must say what each of these constitutions is at slightly greater length. For the matter is not without difficulty; and in every inquiry it is the part of a serious student, who is not merely aiming at practice, to overlook and omit nothing, but display the truth about each thing.

1279ᵇ16. As we have said, tyranny is despotic monarchy in political society, oligarchy is when those who own the property are sovereign, and democracy on the contrary is when those are sovereign who do not possess substantial property but are needy. A first difficulty concerns the definition. If the majority, being prosperous, were sovereign in the city, and democracy is when the mass is sovereign—and similarly if somewhere it may happen that the needy are fewer than the prosperous, but being stronger are sovereign in the State, while oligarchy is said to be where a small body is sovereign—the definitions of the constitutions would not seem right.

1279ᵇ26. If we combine fewness with prosperity and multitude with need, and say that oligarchy is the constitution in which the prosperous hold the offices and are few in number, while democracy is that in which the needy do so and are many in number, another difficulty arises: what are we to call the constitutions just described, that in which the sovereign is a prosperous majority and that in which it is a needy minority, if there are no other constitutions than those named?

1279^{b}34. This discussion seems to make it plain that the sovereign's being few or many is an accident of oligarchies and democracies respectively, due to the prosperous being everywhere few and the needy many (which is why the causes mentioned do not cause a difference). The real difference between democracy and oligarchy is poverty and wealth. Wherever the rulers rule because of their wealth, that must be an oligarchy whether they are few or many, and wherever the needy rule must be a democracy. Only it happens that, as we said, the one party is few and the other many. For few are prosperous, but all enjoy freedom; and each side demands power on one of these grounds.

COMMENT. 'What are we to call the constitutions just described, that in which the sovereign is a prosperous majority and that in which it is a needy minority?' (1279^{b}31). It is plain what we are to call them in terms of the division in III 7. According to that division, if the majority rules for its own advantage, that is a democracy, no matter how rich the majority may be; and if a minority rules for its own advantage, that is an oligarchy, no matter how poor this minority.

But Aristotle now finds himself unwilling to follow the logic of his division in III 7, no doubt because it does not represent the actual use of the words. He had, in fact, already abandoned it by the end of III 7. He now analyses oligarchy and democracy as being essentially the rule of the prosperous and the rule of the needy, and only accidentally, and unessentially, the rule of a few and of a many. This is nearly always his point of view in the rest of the *Politics*. It is certain, therefore, that the *Politics* uses the word 'democracy' to mean something much closer to the rule of the proletariat than to the rule of all.

Thus the one–few–many scheme is dropped as soon as stated, like the doctrine of III 3 that a change of constitution is a change of city. Such alterations of view are frequent in the *Politics*.

He should have dropped also the statement that 'there are no other constitutions than those named' ($1279^{b}33$). If the division in III 7 were exhaustive (which it is not), there would be no other constitutions *on that principle of division*. But no division however good can make it illegal to divide the same genus on another principle also, and thus obtain a different set of species, to which we may then give what new names we please.

III 9–13. JUSTICE

III 9. SUMMARY. *Justice is equals for equals and unequals for unequals. The question is: unequals in what respect? This depends on the purpose of the city. The purpose of the city is not possessions, nor alliance, nor commerce, but goodness and the good life. Hence what counts is inequality in political goodness.*

TRANSLATION. 1280ᵃ7. The first thing to note is what marks men give of oligarchy and democracy, and what are oligarchic and democratic justice.

1280ᵃ9. All men grasp justice to some extent; but they only go part of the way, and they do not state the whole of the absolutely just. For example, justice is thought to be equality; and so it is, but for equals, not for everybody. Inequality is also thought to be just; and so it is, but for unequals, not for everybody. They omit the 'for whom' and judge badly. That is because they are judging about themselves. Most men are bad judges in their own cause.

1280ᵃ16. Justice is relative to persons, and requires the same ratio for the persons as for the things, as was said earlier in the *Ethics*. Men admit the equality of the things but dispute that of the persons. This is mainly because, as just mentioned, they judge badly in their own affairs, but also because each side is really saying something true about justice and hence thinks it is saying the whole truth. The one party, being unequal in some respect, as possessions, thinks itself wholly unequal. The other party, being equal in some respect, as freedom, thinks itself wholly equal.

1280ᵃ25. But they omit the main point. If they came together and made a society for the sake of possessions, then their rights in the city are equal to their property, and the oligarchic argument would seem to have force, since it is not just that he who contributed only one of a hundred pounds should share them equally with him who gave all the rest, or the profits from them. But society exists not for the sake of mere living but rather of living well. Otherwise there could be a city of slaves or of the other animals. There is no such thing because these beings do not enjoy happiness or choose their ways of living. Nor does society exist merely for the sake of alliance, to avoid being wronged by anyone, or because of trade and commerce. If it did, the Etruscans and the Carthaginians, and all who have treaties with each other, would be as citizens of one city, since they have agreements about imports and treaties about refraining from damage and documents about alliance. But they do not have common officers for these matters; each side has its own officers. They do not aim at forming the moral characters of the other side, or at seeing that no person covered by the agreements is unjust or vicious in any way, but only at not wronging each other. Whereas those who aim at a well-conducted society are concerned with political goodness and badness.

1280^{b}6. This makes it clear that a city must concern itself with goodness if it is to be truly and not merely for convenience called a city. Otherwise the community becomes an alliance, differing from the alliances of separated parties only as regards place; and its law becomes a treaty, and 'a guarantor of reciprocal rights' as Lycophron the sophist said, instead of being what makes the citizens good and just men. That this is so is clear from the fact that, if you brought the places together so that the city of the Megarians and that of the Corinthians touched with their walls, it would still not be one city. Nor would it

be so if each gave the other rights of intermarriage,
although this is one of the communisms that are characteristic of cities. Nor would it be so if they lived apart but
not too far apart to have things in common, and had laws
against cheating themselves in exchange, one being say a
carpenter and another a farmer and another a cobbler and
so on, ten thousand in all, but had nothing else in common
beyond such things as alliance and trade.

1280^{b}23. Why is this? It is not because of the dispersion
of the community. Such a community, where they only
helped each other against wrongdoers as in a defensive
alliance, and each man treated his own household like
a city, would not even if they came together seem a city
to accurate observers, if the manner of the association
remained the same. This makes it plain that the city is not
the sharing of a place, and does not exist to prevent wrong
and promote exchange. These are necessary conditions
of there being a city. But a city is not just the presence of
all of them. It is the community of the households and the
clans in the good life, for the sake of perfect and selfsufficient life. But this will not happen unless they inhabit one
and the same place and recognize intermarriages. Hence
the origin of family connexions in the cities and brotherhoods and sacrifices and community gatherings. This
kind of thing is the work of friendship, since voluntary
living together constitutes friendship. The end of a city is
the good life, and these things are for the sake of the end.
A city is the sharing of clans and villages in a perfect and
selfsufficient life. That is, we say, a happy and good life.

1281^{a}2. We must lay it down, therefore, that the purpose
of political society is not living together but good actions.
Hence those who contribute most to such a society have
a larger share in the city than those who are equal or

superior in freedom and birth but unequal in political goodness, or those who are superior in wealth but inferior in goodness.

1281ᵃ8. It is clear from the above that all those who dispute about the constitutions are asserting some part of justice.

COMMENT. Aristotle held that a distribution of goods is just if the ratio of the value of a man's share to the value of the man himself is the same for every man. To put it in mathematical terms, justice is done if, for any two men A and B, A is to A's share as B is to B's share. A/A's share = B/B's share. As he said, justice is proportionate equality, not simple equality.

In politics the main good to be distributed is office and power. The just city, therefore, is the city where every man's share of office and power stands in the same ratio as every other man's to his personal value. A's power always ought to be to A's value just as B's power is to B's value. This must be made to hold for every pair of citizens if the city is to be just.

What constitutes the personal value of the men in this equation? How do we tell whether A is more valuable than B? Aristotle says in this chapter that, for the purpose of distributing offices, the relevant value is not a man's wealth or freedom or birth, but his 'political goodness'. Hence, finally, the just city is that in which the ratio of a man's political power to his political goodness is always the same.

But what is political goodness? Aristotle does not explain. He seems to think the meaning of the phrase well known to his readers; but it is obscure to us today. In 1280ᵇ5 political goodness looks like good character and good behaviour towards the city and its laws and citizens. In 1281ᵃ7 it looks like the power to produce good character and good behaviour in the other citizens. The latter is probably Aristotle's idea: political goodness is being good at making men good by ruling them.

Why is political goodness what decides how much power a man should have? Because the end of a city is the good life (1280ᵇ39). We do not learn much in this chapter about the good life, only that it is 'perfect and selfsufficient' (1280ᵇ34) and 'happy and good' and consists in 'good actions' (1281ᵃ2). There is a long discussion of it in VII 1-3, from which I extract the following. The good life involves having good possessions and a good body; but it consists mainly in having a good soul and acting well. That is, it consists mainly in being virtuous and doing virtuous acts, including the acts of courage, temperance, justice, and wisdom. Good action may be political action, ruling over others. But it is certainly not despotic or imperial rule, as it is often supposed to be. And it need not have any relation to other persons. It may be just contemplation and reflection for its own sake (1325ᵇ20).

The train of thought is therefore as follows. The end of the city is the good life. Therefore the ruler should be the man who can produce the good life. But the good life is mainly the practice of the various goodnesses or virtues. Therefore the ruler should be the man who can make the citizens practise goodness. But making the citizens good by ruling them is what we call 'political goodness'. Therefore his political goodness is the correct criterion of a man's right to rule.

Thus it is, according to Aristotle, an essential function of the city to make the citizens virtuous and well behaved. It would not really be a city at all if it did not have this aim, but confined itself like a commercial alliance to the regulation of transactions and the prevention of unfair practices. The end of the city is the good life.

Thus Aristotle is not a liberal, if liberalism includes the doctrine that the State should confine itself to protecting the citizens against aggression and deception and theft, and should not try to mould their characters further than this entails. We might say he is a paternalist, defining paternalism as the doctrine that the State should try to make its citizens virtuous as parents should try to make their children virtuous.

He deduces his paternalism from the premiss that 'the end of a city is the good life' (1280ᵇ39). How does he know this premiss? The chapter contains much argument for it, but argument that appeals only to those already converted. The city, he says, is neither an alliance nor a community of place; and everyone will agree with that. Therefore, he infers, it is a community for the good life and aims at that. But this does not follow. And his suggestion that this is part of the meaning of the word 'city' is false (1280ᵇ7). What makes the difference between a city and an alliance or a contiguity is that the city is administered by one set of sovereign officers, as he himself really knows (1280ᵇ1); the end which the city sets before itself has nothing to do with it.

Professor Havelock considered this chapter to contain 'as dishonest a piece of interpretation as can be found anywhere in [Aristotle's] pages'; and that meant very dishonest, in view of the hate and contempt of Aristotle's politics which Professor Havelock revealed. The dishonesty consisted in concealing or distorting a doctrine of whose existence Aristotle was aware, namely the 'serious theoretic position that men are historically equal and should be socially organized in such a way as to reflect this' (*The Liberal Temper in Greek Politics*, New Haven, 1957, p. 371). Professor Havelock implied, I think, that there existed some political treatise as serious and sophisticated as Aristotle's, but taking a contrary view on equality, and that Aristotle was here dishonestly giving a false account of this treatise.

This is grossly distorted. Aristotle is not giving any 'interpretation' at all in this chapter, and hence cannot be giving a dishonest interpretation. He is merely referring to the wide and vague claims of equality often made in political argument, and indicating how in his opinion they require to be limited and specified. So much is certain. It is also probable, in my opinion, that no such 'serious theoretic' treatise existed; but, even if it did exist, and Aristotle knew of it and did not mention it here, that does not make him dishonest. There is no duty to state the opposing position every time that one states one's own.

III 10. SUMMARY. *Should the sovereign be the masses, or the rich, or the good, or the one best man, or a tyrant? There are objections to all of them.*

TRANSLATION. 1281ª11. It is a problem who should be the sovereign in the city. Apparently it must be either the masses, or the rich, or the good, or the one best man, or a tyrant. But all of them seem unacceptable. What if the poor because they are a majority distribute the property of the rich, is not that unjust? 'Certainly not, if it was justly decided by the sovereign.' But, if that is not the limit of injustice, what is? And if, when everything has been taken, the majority again distribute the goods of the minority, they obviously ruin the city. But goodness does not ruin its possessor; and justice is not destructive of a city. Plainly, therefore, this law cannot be just. Besides which, it would necessarily make just everything the tyrant did; in compelling because he is the stronger, he behaves as the masses do towards the rich.

1281ᵃ24. Is it then just that the minority and the rich should rule? If then they too act in this way, snatching and confiscating the property of the majority, this is just. Then so is the other. It is clear that these arrangements are all bad and not just.

1281ᵃ28. Then should the good hold office and be the supreme sovereign? If so, everyone else will be excluded from office, and so will be dishonoured. For office is honour, we say; and, if the officers are always the same men, everyone else is necessarily without honour.

1281ᵃ32. Then is it better that the one best man should rule? But that is even more oligarchical, since it leaves more persons without honour.

1281ᵃ34. Perhaps someone will say that for the sovereign to be a man at all and not law is bad, since he will have the passions that beset the soul. But law will not solve the problem if it is oligarchic or democratic law; the same consequences will arise as were mentioned before.

COMMENT. Aristotle asks who *ought* to be the sovereign in a State. In the nineteenth century men asked who *was* the sovereign in each State. They conceived of the sovereign as being the supreme officer who gave orders to others and took no orders from others. It was on the model of an army where the private soldier only takes orders and never gives any, most ranks both take orders from above and give them to those below, and the commanding officer only gives orders and never takes them. The problem was to find who corresponded to such a commanding officer in some contemporary State. They did not admit the possibility that the State did not resemble an army and had no sovereign. Even where the State had been intentionally constructed so as not to have a sovereign, they still insisted on finding one there. Thus they reached conclusions like 'the sovereign in the United States is a two-thirds majority of the States', which is selfcontradictory because a sovereign is an officer but a two-thirds majority is not an officer.

Aristotle's question is who *ought* to be sovereign. The right answer is that there ought to be *no* sovereign in a State. The good State does not have a sovereign, but arranges so that all officers take orders as well as give them, thus protecting the citizens against the corrupting effect on officers of untrammelled power. But this never became clear to the ancient Greeks, though Aristotle makes a great advance towards it in the following chapters.

There is a second error in the question 'Who ought to be sovereign?'. This is that it carries with it the question 'Who ought to be the chief executive?', and this implies that a constitution should include a rule which automatically determines who is the chief executive at all times. Such are the rules that 'the chief executive shall always be the eldest son of the previous chief executive', and that 'the chief executive shall always be the five thousand richest men'. But all such rules are undesirable. The constitution should contain a rule saying who are to be the electors of the chief executive, and how long they are to elect him for, but not a rule indicating precisely whom they are to elect. The automatic element should bear on the electors of the executive, not on the executive himself.

Aristotle's own answer will be in terms of law. But he does not give it in this chapter. Law is not among the possible answers contemplated in the second sentence. It is introduced at the end, but, like the previous answers, it is dismissed with a difficulty. The chapter is, in fact, a pure example of aporetic procedure, with negative result. It raises a question, mentions several conceivable answers, and objects to all of them.

There is a slight insincerity in this aporetic procedure. Aristotle does not really think that law can be thus dismissed. Even his previous argument against making the good men sovereign is probably one to which he himself attaches little weight. Perhaps he also saw that even his arguments against the poor or the rich being sovereign are weak, because they merely point out that these rulers may act unjustly, and any ruler however chosen may act unjustly. But he accepts this slight insincerity in order to put us into a properly wondering and open frame of mind to receive the true answer later. It is the insincerity of the teacher getting his pupils to reflect on the matter by pretending to be puzzled himself. In this respect it resembles the slyness or 'irony' of the Socratic method of teaching depicted by Plato. The logical skeleton is, however, quite different, since there is no syllogizing here.

III 11. SUMMARY. *The masses should share in deliberation and judgement, but not in the highest offices. The supreme authority should be the laws.*

TRANSLATION. 1281ᵃ39. The rest of these views may be discussed at another time; but the view that the masses rather than the few best men should be sovereign would seem to be held and to contain some difficulty and perhaps some truth. For the many, none of whom is a good man, may nevertheless be better than the few good men when they get together. Not that each by himself will be better but that as a whole they will be, as meals to which many have contributed are better than those provided by one outlay. For each of these many may possess some part of goodness and wisdom; and when they get together, as the mass may be a single man with many feet and many hands and many senses, so it may be with their character and thought. That is why the many are better judges of works of music and poetry; some judge one part, some another, and all together they judge it all. Where the good differ from each one of the many is the same as where they say beautiful people differ from those who are not beautiful, and artistic representations of objects from the objects themselves, namely in uniting into one things scattered and separate. In separation somebody may have an eye more beautiful than the pictured eye, and somebody else another part more beautiful.

1281ᵇ15. It is not clear that *every* demos and *every* majority can excel the few good men in this way. Or, rather, it is pretty clear that some of them cannot; for the same argument would apply to beasts—and some men hardly differ from beasts. But what has been said may perfectly well be true of *some* majority.

1281ᵇ21. These considerations suffice to solve not merely

the above problem but also the connected problem what the free men and the mass of the citizens should be sovereign over. These are those who are not rich and have no claim whatever to goodness. It is unsafe for them to share in the highest offices, for their injustice and folly would inevitably lead them into crimes and mistakes. But it is dangerous to allow them no share at all, for a city in which there are many poor men excluded from office must be full of enemies. The remaining alternative is for them to share in deliberation and judgement. That is why Solon and some other legislators assign to them the election and the audit of the officers, but do not let them hold office singly. Their perceptions are adequate for this when they are all together, and when mixed with the better sort they benefit the cities, just as a mixture of concentrated and other food is more useful than a little of the concentrated food alone; but individually each of them makes an imperfect judge.

1281^{b}38. Yet there are difficulties in this disposition of the constitution. (1) In the first place, it would seem that the same person should judge who has treated a disease correctly as should treat it when present and restore the patient to health; and this is the physician. And the same with the other arts and crafts. As therefore a physician should be examined by physicians, so also the others should be by their peers. (The physician may be either a practitioner or a director or a person learned in the art. This third class exists in practically every art; and we hold that it is as capable of judging as the experts are.) It would seem, furthermore, that the same applies to choosing officers. Correct choice is a job for those who know: choice of a geometer for those who know geometry, of a navigator for those who know navigation. Even if for some technical posts some laymen share in the choice, at any rate they do not do so more than the experts. Thus this line of thought implies that the masses should not be given either the election or the audit of officers.

1282ᵃ14. But perhaps this is not wholly correct, for two reasons. According to the previous argument, although each by himself is a worse judge than the experts, yet all together they will be no worse or even better (unless they happen to be a hopelessly slavish lot). And, secondly, in some cases the maker might not be the only or even the best judge, namely where persons who lack the skill are nevertheless familiar with the products. Thus the maker is not the only one who knows about a house; he who uses it, the householder, is an even better judge of it, and so is a helmsman a better judge of a rudder than a carpenter, and the guest of a feast, not the cook. This might perhaps be thought a sufficient answer to the present difficulty.

1282ᵃ24. (2) There is, however, another difficulty connected with this. It seems absurd that bad men should control greater matters than good men; yet the audits and elections of officers are the greatest matter, and in some constitutions, as has been said, they are assigned to the demos, the assembly being in control of all such matters. Yet a small amount of property, and any age whatever, entitle a man to be an assemblyman and a councillor and a judge, whereas it requires much property to be treasurer or general or any of the greatest officers.

1282ᵃ32. This difficulty could also be solved in the same way. Here, too, perhaps, the arrangement is correct. For the officer is not the judge or the councillor or the assemblyman but the court and the council and the demos; each of the persons mentioned is a part of these, I mean the councillor, the assemblyman, and the judge. Hence it is just for the mass to control greater matters, since the demos and the council and the court consist of many persons, the property-qualification of whom, taken all together, is greater than that of those who fill great offices individually or in small groups. Let these matters be determined in this way.

1282^{b}1. Nothing emerges so clearly from the first mentioned difficulty as that the supreme authority ought to be the laws correctly established, and that the ruler, whether one or many, ought to have authority over such matters as the laws are quite unable to determine precisely owing to its not being easy to decide everything in general terms. Of what sort, however, these correctly established laws ought to be is by no means plain as yet. On the contrary, the old difficulty remains: the laws will inevitably be bad or good, and just or unjust, concomitantly with the constitutions. Only this much is clear: the laws should suit the constitution. From this, however, it plainly follows that laws matching the correct constitutions must be just, and those matching the perverted ones not just.

COMMENT. The chapter expounds an important consideration in favour of democracy, including our kind of democracy as well as Aristotle's. He makes clear what is wrong with the argument that government should be left to experts, because it is an art or craft, and no art is the possession of people *en masse*. He does not deny that government is an art, or that no art is the possession of a majority; on the contrary, he by implication accepts these propositions. But he affirms that the public is sometimes a better judge of artists and their products than are the artists themselves, and that this applies to the art of government as much as to that of music.

He puts it always in terms of judging what is objectively good or bad. He does not use the argument that the public has a right to choose whichever artists it subjectively prefers. He never says that the public is entitled to choose the rulers who will give it the kind of city it prefers. He cannot say that because according to him the end of government is objectively fixed, and hence not open to choice by individual peoples. Yet in Book V of the *Politics* he gives advice on how to establish and maintain any kind of constitution you wish to have.

The argument, that the user is a better judge of a product than is the maker of it, had been employed by Plato to disparage painters as ignoramuses (*Republic* X 601–2). Plato would not have been pleased to hear it employed in favour of letting the common people choose and criticize their rulers.

As in the previous chapter, the discussion of law is postponed to the last paragraph and is very slight, though now a little less slight than before. Aristotle does, however, clearly enunciate the very important principle that 'the supreme authority ought to be the laws correctly established'. In other words, there should be no officer not bound by laws; even the supreme executive should be subject to them. It is not clear why he thinks that this emerges from his discussion.

'The elections and the audits of the officers.' The Athenian 'audit' was an examination of officers, at the end of their term, on their conduct in office, and was a common feature of the constitution. Any person could make a charge against an officer to the auditors. This institution shows that the Athenians had a strong feeling that power corrupts, and at the same time it explains why Aristotle feels no particular need to insist on the fact that power corrupts. He tells us that the Spartan Elders, who were not subject to audit, took bribes and did favours (1271ª3–6).

It is an interesting question why twentieth-century democracies have no such institution, and whether it would benefit them. Perhaps it ought to be easier than it is to prosecute modern prosecutors and policemen and Home Secretaries for their conduct of their offices. When an English judge tells a jury that it is no concern of theirs whether the police obtained their evidence legally, something seems to be very wrong. On the other hand, the Athenian demos exercised 'a veritable tyranny over the officers' (Glotz, p. 268); and Thucydides believed that the Athenian army in Sicily was lost because Nicias thought he would be impeached if he retreated (VII 48).

III 12. SUMMARY. *Political justice is equality in rule proportionate not to wealth or birth or freedom, but to contribution to the city.*

TRANSLATION. 1282ᵇ14. In all the sciences and arts the end is a good. Greatest and most good is the end of the most sovereign of them all, which is political ability. The political good is justice, and that is the common advantage.

1282ᵇ18. All men hold that justice is some kind of equality; and up to a certain point they agree with what has been determined in our philosophical discussions on ethical matters. That is, they say that justice is a certain distribution to certain persons, and must be equal for equals. What we have to discover is equality and inequality of what sort of persons. That is difficult, and calls for political philosophy.

1282ᵇ23. Perhaps someone would say that superiority in any good whatever deserves inequality in the assignment of offices, provided that in all other respects the men do not differ but are alike, on the ground that whoever differs has a different right and worth. But, if this is true, complexion and height and any good whatever will entitle those who excel in it to an excess of political rights. But is not this obviously false? That it is so is plain from the other sciences and abilities. Among fluteplayers who are equal in the art we should not give the preference of flutes to the more nobly born, because they will not play any better. We should give the superiority in instruments to him who is superior at the work. If the point is not yet clear, it will be made plain by developing it even further. If someone excelled at playing the flute, but was very inferior in birth or beauty, then, even if each of these is a greater good than fluteplaying (I mean birth and beauty), and even if their superiority to fluteplaying is proportionately greater than his superiority as a fluteplayer, still he should be given the outstanding flutes. For the superiority must contribute to the work; but superiority in wealth and birth contribute nothing.

1283ᵃ3. Furthermore, this principle would make every

good comparable with every other good. For, if a certain height counted, then height in general would count, both as compared with wealth and as compared with freedom. Consequently, if one man differs from another in height more than the other differs from him in goodness, then, even if in general goodness excels height, everything would be comparable. For, plainly, if this much is better than that much, some other amount is equal thereto.

1283ᵃ9. Since this is impossible, it is clear that in politics also it is reasonable not to claim office on the ground of any and every inequality. Differences in speed, for example, do not entitle a person to more political power; they get their reward in athletic competitions. The claim must be based on a difference in something that helps to constitute a city. Hence it is reasonable for the noble and free and rich to claim the honour, because the citizens must be free and have taxable property; a city could not consist entirely of needy persons, any more than of slaves. And, if those attributes are necessary, evidently justice and political goodness are necessary too. Without these, also, a city cannot go on. Or, rather, without the former, it cannot exist, and without these it cannot go on well.

COMMENT. This chapter repeats, though less distinctly, the point of III 9, that the criterion of fitness to rule is 'political goodness' (1283ᵃ20).

'Justice . . . is the common advantage.' This doctrine has a much more liberal sound than his other doctrine that the end of the city is the good life, where 'good' tends to mean virtuous. Is it the end of the city that everybody shall receive some advantage, or that everybody shall be virtuous, or both? Aristotle does not explicitly decide the point; but he writes nearly always on the assumption that the end of the city is that everybody shall be virtuous. The doctrine that justice is the common advantage, though uttered more than once, has mainly the negative purpose of condemning all rule by a party for its own advantage. On the positive side it is overridden by the doctrine that the aim of the city is the good or virtuous life.

III 13. SUMMARY. *The principles on which men claim to rule are all incorrect; for, whichever of these principles we adopt, it follows that, if one party or one man is supreme in respect of that principle, he ought to rule alone. This difficulty is most acute when goodness is held to be what justifies rule. If there is one man whose goodness is beyond comparison with that of the rest, it is ridiculous to make laws for him. Laws are for equals; and the purpose of ostracism in democratic cities is to get rid of those who have much more power than the rest. The problem applies to all constitutions, including the correct ones. Perhaps we should say that, when someone becomes outstanding in goodness, the only thing to do is to make him king and gladly obey him.*

TRANSLATION. 1283ª23. For the mere existence of a city all or at any rate some of these would appear to have a proper claim; but for good life education and goodness would have the most just claim, as has been said before. And since equality in one point does not call for equality in all, and inequality in one point does not call for inequality in all, all such constitutions must be perversions. Now I have said before that, while all the claims are just to some extent, they are not all absolutely just. The rich are right in that they have a larger share in the land and the land is a public concern, also in that they are usually more reliable in business dealings. The free and the noble are right in the respect in which they are near together: the noble are citizens to a greater degree than the ignoble, and nobility is always honoured in its own country. Also because the sons of better men are likely to be better, since nobility is goodness of stock. Similarly, we shall say that the claim of goodness is also just; for justice according to us is social goodness, and on it all the other goodnesses must follow. The majority are also right in their claim against the minority, since when taken together they are stronger and richer and better than the few.

1283ᵃ42. We may ask, therefore, whether, if they were all present in one city, I mean both the good and the rich and the noble, and a mass of citizens in addition, there will or will not be dispute as to who should rule. According to each of the constitutions we have described, the decision who should rule is indisputable. For it is precisely in their rulers that they differ from each other. For example, one of them is rule by the rich, another rule by the good men, and so on for all the rest. But nevertheless let us consider what we are to say when these parties are all present at the same time. If the good men were extremely few in number, how ought we to settle it? Surely their fewness must be considered with reference to the work. Are they enough to be able to administer the city? Are they so many in number as to compose a city?

1283ᵇ13. There is a certain difficulty that confronts all claims for political honours. It would seem that wealth gives no right to rule, and birth gives none either. For if there is one man who is richer than all of them, then obviously by the same right he ought to rule alone. Similarly, he who excels in birth should be the sole ruler of those who claim on the ground of their freedom. And perhaps the same thing will occur even in aristocracies with regard to goodness; if there were one man who was better than the other good men in the government, he should rule by the same right. Similarly, if the masses should rule because they are stronger than the few, then, if there were one man, or a number of persons more than one but fewer than the many, who were stronger than the rest, they ought to rule rather than the masses.

1283ᵇ27. All these things seem to make it plain that these marks, in virtue of which men demand to rule and to be obeyed by everyone else, are all incorrect. Even against those who demand control of the government on account of their goodness, just as against those who do so on account of their wealth, the masses might have a fair argument; for it may happen some time that the masses are better and richer than the few, not individually but collectively.

1283ᵇ35. Hence we can meet in this way the difficulty which people often seek to put forward, namely whether a lawgiver who wishes to make the most correct laws should look to the advantage of the better sort or of the majority, in the case mentioned. Perhaps we should ask what constitutes correctness here. That is correct, perhaps, which is to the advantage of the whole city and to the common advantage of the citizens. A citizen is everywhere he who shares in ruling and being ruled, but how he does so varies with each constitution. In the best constitution he is the man who both can and does rule and obey with the intention of achieving the life of goodness.

1284ᵃ3. If there is one man who differs so much in excess of goodness (or more than one, who are nevertheless not enough to fill up a city) that there is no comparison between the goodness and political ability of all the other persons and theirs, if there is more than one of them (or his, if he is only one), then they must no longer be reckoned as part of a city. For it will be wrong to expect them to submit to equal shares, when they are so unequal in goodness and political ability. Such a man is presumably like a god among men. Hence it is plain that lawgiving too must concern itself with those who are equal both in kind and in ability. For such men as these there is no law; they themselves are law. Anyone who tried to legislate for them would be ridiculous; and they would probably say what according to Antisthenes the lions said when the hares

were orating and demanding equality for everybody.[1]
That is why democratic cities establish ostracism, namely
for some such reason as this: they appear to aim at equality
above all things, and so they used to ostracize, and expel
from the city for a limited time, those who appeared to
have too much power, owing to wealth or influence or any
other political strength. The myth tells that it was for such
a reason also that the Argonauts left Heracles behind; the
Argo refused to carry him with the other voyagers, as
being much in excess. Hence those who censure the
tyranny and the advice of Periander to Thrasybulus
should not be considered correct without qualification.
The story is that Periander said nothing to the messenger
who had been sent to him for advice, but levelled the
field by taking away the outstanding ears. The messenger
did not know why he did so, but, when he reported what
had happened, Thrasybulus understood that he should
get rid of the outstanding men.

1284ª33. Tyrants are not the only ones who benefit by
this policy and follow it. The same is true of oligarchies
also and of democracies. For the effect of ostracism is in
a way the same as that of docking and banishing the
outstanding men. Those who are in power do the same
with cities and nations. The Athenians did so with the
Samians and Chians and Lesbians: once they had their
empire under control, they humbled them contrary to the
treaties. And the king of the Persians often cut down
Medes and Babylonians and whoever else presumed on
having once been in power.

1284ᵇ3. The problem applies generally to all constitutions, including the correct ones. The perverted ones do
it with a view to their private good; but the same thing

---

[1] They said: 'Where are your claws and teeth?'

happens in those aiming at the common good. It is plain to see in the other arts and sciences also. No painter would let his figure have a disproportionately large foot, however outstanding in beauty, no shipbuilder such a poop or other part of the ship. Nor will the producer accept a singer whose voice is stronger and better than the whole company. As far as this goes, therefore, a monarch may accord perfectly well with his city, if, while he acts in this way, his rule is useful to the city. Hence for acknowledged superiorities there is some political justice in the argument about ostracism. It is indeed better if the lawgiver in the beginning so composes the constitution that it does not need such a remedy; but the next best thing is, if the occasion arises, to try to correct it by some such correction. However, this is not what happened with the cities. They did not look to the advantage of their own constitution, but used the ostracisms for party purposes.

1284^{b}22. In the perverted constitutions, therefore, it is plain that ostracism is for private purposes useful and right; but perhaps it is also plain that it is not right absolutely speaking. But in the best constitution it is very difficult to know what to do, not indeed about superiority in other goods like strength and wealth and influence, but when someone becomes outstanding in personal goodness. One certainly would not say that such a man should be expelled and removed. Yet nor can one exercise authority over such a man; for that would be like dividing the offices and claiming authority over God. The remaining possibility, which seems to be the natural one, is for everyone gladly to obey such a man, and for such men to be perpetual kings in the cities.

COMMENT. In III 10–12 Aristotle seemed to be slowly and aporetically working towards advising the rule of law. And so he is, upon the whole. But he admits one possible exception: the outstandingly good man, so good that there is no comparison between him and the rest, like a god among men. He feels that it would be ridiculous and impossible to impose the rule of law on such a man; the only thing to do would be to make him king and gladly obey him. He means an absolute king, not subject to any constitutional law.

There are several questions we should like to ask Aristotle about this: Has such a man ever appeared? Is Alexander such a man? What is to be done when some of the citizens say that such a man has appeared and others deny it? What is to be done if the citizens, having believed they had such a man and voted him the kingship for life, now think he is not an outstandingly good man? What is to be done at the death of such a man? Will the previous constitution be automatically in force again? But there is nothing to show for certain how Aristotle would have replied.

One thing is certain, however, namely that this is a real and permanent belief of Aristotle's, not merely an argument inserted to make us think. It is probably inconsistent with some other beliefs of his; but Aristotle did worship, or at least look up to with awed respect, some ideally highminded or 'megalopsychic' person who 'demands great honours and deserves them' (*Nic. Eth.* IV 3). He is not intending either to joke or to puzzle us, either here or in his account of the megalopsychic man in the *Ethics*.

III 14–18. KING OR LAW?

III 14. SUMMARY. *There are five kinds of kingship: (1) the Spartan, a sort of hereditary and permanent generalship; (2) the barbaric, that is, hereditary, despotic, but legal rule; (3) aesymnety, that is, elected tyranny; (4) the heroic, which was legal and traditional and by consent; (5) when one man controls everything, as if the city were his household.*

TRANSLATION. 1284ᵇ35. It may be well to leave the matters just discussed and examine kingship, which we hold to be one of the correct constitutions. We must ask whether having a king suits a city and country that is to do well, or whether, on the contrary, some other constitution is better, or whether it suits some cities but not others.

1284ᵇ40. The first thing to determine is whether there is more than one kind of kingship. It is easy to see that it includes several kinds, and that the manner of rule is not identical in all.

1285ᵃ3. (1) In the Spartan constitution the office is thought to be more of a kingship than in any other legal example. The king is not, however, in control of everything; but when he leaves the country he is the leader in military matters. Religious affairs are also allotted to the kings. This kingship is like a sort of generalship with absolute powers, and is held for life. He has no power to put to death, except for cowardice and on the field, as in military expeditions in ancient times. Homer shows this; for Agamemnon when abused endured it in the assemblies, but in the field he had the power even to kill. Thus he says: 'Whom I find apart from battle . . . there will be no surety for him to escape dogs and ominous birds; for with me is death.' This then is one sort of kingship, namely generalship for life. Some of them are hereditary and others elective.

1285ᵃ16. (2) Besides this there is another sort of monarchy, such as the kingships found among some of the barbarians. These are all like tyrannies in their powers, but they are legal and traditional. Barbarians being by nature more slavish in character than Greeks, and those in Asia more so than those in Europe, they endure despotic rule without distaste. Thus these monarchies are tyrannical in this respect, but they are secure because they are traditional and legal. Also the guard is royal and not tyrannical for the same reason. The armed guards of kings are citizens, but those of tyrants are foreign. This is because the former rule legally over consenting subjects, but the latter over unwilling ones; and hence the former maintain a guard from the citizens but the latter against the citizens. We have now two sorts of monarchy.

1285ᵃ30. (3) Another is what used to exist among the ancient Greeks, what they call *aesymnetes*. That is, to speak broadly, elected tyranny, differing from the barbaric not in not being legal but only in not being traditional. This office was held sometimes for life and sometimes for a determinate period or action. Thus the Mytilenians once chose Pittacus against the exiles who were led by Antimenides and Alcaeus the poet. Alcaeus shows that they chose Pittacus as tyrant in one of his table-songs, where he complains that 'baseborn Pittacus they made tyrant of the gentle and luckless city and thronged to exalt him'.

1285ᵇ2. The above forms are and were tyrannical in being despotic, but kingly in being elected and by consent. (4) A fourth kind of kingly monarchy consists of those in heroic times which were both legal and traditional and by consent. Because they benefited the masses in the arts or in war, or because they brought them together or provided land, the founders became kings by consent and a tradition to their successors. They controlled the command in war and such sacrifices as were not sacerdotal, and in addition they decided the lawsuits. Some of them did this without and some with an oath; the oath was a raising of the sceptre. In ancient times they governed continuously both city and country and foreign affairs. But later the kings themselves dropped some things, and the masses took others away, and in some cities only the sacrifices were left to the kings. Where something worth calling kingship remained, they only had the command in war beyond the frontiers.

1285ᵇ20. These then are forms of kingship, four in number. One is that of the heroic age; this was by consent, but on certain definite terms; the king was general and judge, and he controlled relations with the gods. A second is the barbaric, that is, hereditary, despotic, legal rule. A third is what they designate as aesymnety, that is, elected tyranny. And fourth among them is the Spartan, that is, broadly speaking, hereditary perpetual generalship. These forms differ from each other in this way.

1285ᵇ29. (5) A fifth form of kingship is when one man controls everything just as each nation and each city controls its public affairs. This is parallel to household management. As household management is a sort of kingship in a house, so this kingship is a household management of a city and of one or more nations.

COMMENT. In III 6–7 Aristotle divided the constitution into six kinds of constitution. He now subdivides one of these six, namely kingship, into five subkinds. The subdivision comes upon us unexpectedly and seems to break the train of thought. It is also rather unmethodically done. Four constitutions are described. Then their descriptions are briefly repeated in a different order, for no apparent reason. Then a fifth is described.

In the next book the other constitutions are subdivided, equally unmethodically. Aristotle finds five (or four) subkinds of democracy, four subkinds of oligarchy, four subkinds of aristocracy, and three subkinds of tyranny. He does not subdivide 'constitutional' government. Thus he finally has twenty-one or twenty-two subkinds of constitution.

There is a noticeable difference between the first division in III 6–7 and the subsequent subdivisions. The first division was logical, made according to two clearly stated principles of division, one into two parts and the other into three parts, which by their multiplication gave six constitutions; and this division claimed to be exhaustive on principle.

The subdivisions, on the other hand, are empirical, not logical. Gustav Glotz was wrong to say, in his excellent *La Cité Grecque*, p. 80, that Aristotle's subdivision of oligarchy is purely logical and hence artificial. He himself disproves this incidental mistake by going on to give copious illustrations of Aristotle's subtypes of oligarchy. Aristotle is describing differences which he has observed. If the result is exhaustive, it is so because Aristotle has seen everything, not because some concept has been logically divided. Indeed, we who have not had Aristotle's experience, but can only go by his descriptions, are sometimes unable to see a clear difference between what he presents as two distinct subforms. The most extraordinary case of this is his presenting the same two forms here as forms of kingship but in IV 10 as forms of tyranny.

These two ambivalent forms, at once kingships and tyrannies, are also the clearest evidence of the truth that Aristotle in making these subdivisions disregards and overrides the principles of his original division. Nothing is said about the question whether the ruler rules for his own or for the public advantage, which was one of the two original principles. Even the one–few–many principle seems to be almost forgotten in some of the accounts of democracies. Aristotle likes to make divisions, but he does not like to abide by them!

We thus receive a strong impression of a more Platonic, more conceptual, division, on which has been imposed a more historical, more empirical, subdivision, resulting in considerable incoherence. This is part of the evidence for Werner Jaeger's theory, in his *Aristotle*, that Aristotle's thinking became more empirical as his life went on.

It appears from the beginning of the next chapter that the fifth subkind of kingship is 'total kingship'; and it appears from 1287ᵃ9 in III 16 that 'total kingship . . . is when the king governs everything as he pleases'. Aristotle means that the 'total king' is not bound by any law (cf. 1287ᵃ3).

Which of these subkinds of kingship is the one that would be exemplified by the 'god among men' of the previous chapter? It must be the fifth; but Aristotle does not say so.

III 15. SUMMARY. *Is it better to be ruled by the best man or by the best laws? The best man would have to promulgate some laws. Matters which the law cannot decide are on the whole decided better by a plurality of good men than by a single one.*

TRANSLATION. 1285ᵇ33. This and the Spartan kind of kingship are about the only two we need consider, since most of the others are between them, in that the king controls less than in the total kingship but more than in the Spartan. Thus there are roughly two questions: first, whether or not it is good for cities to have a perpetual general, either hereditary or elective, and, second, whether or not it is good that one man should be in control of everything. However, the generalship falls under a study of laws rather than of constitutions, since it can occur in all the constitutions; and may therefore be dropped for the present. The remaining sort of kingship is a species of constitution, and hence we must consider it and run over the problems which it raises.

1286ᵃ7. The first thing to ask is this: Is it more advantageous to be governed by the best man or the best laws?

1286ᵃ9. Those who think it advantageous to be ruled by a king hold that law is merely general. It does not deal with particular occasions. That is why in every art it is foolish to go by the book. It is a good thing that in Egypt the physicians are allowed to change after the fourth day. (If he does so earlier, it is at his own risk.) Hence it is plain that, for the same reason, the best constitution does not follow writings and laws.

1286ª16. On the other side, the rulers must have the general principle as well. Furthermore, that to which no emotion whatever attaches is better than that to which emotion is congenital; and the law has no emotion, whereas every human soul must have it. Perhaps someone would reply that on the other hand he will deliberate better about particular cases. Anyhow, it is plain that he must be a lawgiver and have laws; but they must not be sovereign where they err, though they should be sovereign on other matters.

1286ª24. As to matters which the law cannot decide at all, or cannot decide well, should the one best man determine them or everybody? As things are, they come together and judge and deliberate and decide, and these decisions are all about particular cases. Individually, perhaps, the contribution of each is poor; but the city is composed of many of them, as a feast to which many contribute is better than just one. That is why a crowd is a better judge of many things than any one person whatsoever.

1286ª31. Furthermore, the large quantity is less corruptible. As with a larger quantity of water, so also the masses are less corruptible than the few. When a single man is overcome by anger or some other such passion his judgement is inevitably corrupted; but it is a job to make them all angry and mistaken together.

1286ª36. Let the masses be the free men, and let them do nothing outside the law except what the law inevitably omits. Granting that this is not easy when there are many persons, still, if there were a plurality who were both good men and good citizens, which would be the less corruptible ruler, the single man, or rather the plurality who were all good? Clearly the plurality.

1286^{b}1. 'But they will have dissensions, which he will not.' Against this perhaps we must assume that they are good in soul, as he, the one, is too.

1286^{b}3. If the rule of several persons who are all good is to be called aristocracy, and that of the one kingship, then aristocracy would be preferable to kingship in the cities, whether their rule was with or without force, provided that it was possible to get a plurality who were alike. And this is perhaps the reason why there formerly used to be kings, namely that it was hard to find men very outstanding in goodness, especially as cities were small at that time. Also, they made men kings for their beneficence, which is the work of good men. When, however, there began to be many who were alike in goodness, they would no longer put up with a king; instead they looked for something common and established a constitution. And when they grew worse and made money out of public affairs, it was from this presumably that oligarchies arose; they made wealth an object of honour. From these oligarchies they changed first to tyrannies, and from the tyrannies to democracy; for by constantly lessening the governing body out of cupidity they strengthened the masses, who finally set upon them and established democracies. Now that cities have become even larger, it is perhaps no longer easy for any constitution to arise other than democracy.

1286^{b}22. If someone should decide that kingship is the best thing for cities, what is to be done with regard to the children? Is the family as such to rule? But that will be harmful when they turn out as some have done. 'In that case the father, being sovereign, will not give them the kingship.' That is not easy to believe; such an action is difficult, and demands greater goodness than human nature admits.

1286ᵇ27. There is also a problem about power, whether the king should have some force about him with which he can compel those who do not wish to obey. It seems that he cannot rule without it; for, even if his command were legal, and he did nothing at his own pleasure contrary to law, it would still be necessary for him to have power with which to protect the laws.

1286ᵇ34. To decide about this kind of king is probably not difficult: he must have force; but it must be such as to be stronger than each individual and than several of them together, but weaker than the mass, like the guards which the ancients gave when they appointed someone whom they called aesymnete or tyrant of the city, or those which someone advised the Syracusans to give to Dionysius when he asked for the guards.

COMMENT. An intensely aporetic chapter. Aristotle refuses just as coyly as Plato ever did to tell us what to believe. After putting his question (1286ᵃ9) he reports an argument sometimes used in favour of being governed by the one best man (1286ᵃ9–16). Then he gives a reply to this (in 1286ᵃ16–20), which looks more likely to be his own opinion, though it hardly agrees with his recommendation elsewhere of the 'god among men'. Then he reports a continuation of the argument in favour of being governed by the one best man (1286ᵃ20–21). Then he gives what looks rather like his own conclusion from this debate (1286ᵃ21–24): the one best man as ruler will in any case have to promulgate laws, but they must not bind himself where they err. This is consistent with his recommendation of the 'god among men'. But then he devotes the rest and the major part of the chapter to arguing against kingship! So what are we to think? I can only imagine him replying: 'You are to think for yourselves. I have, as I said I would in 1286ᵃ6, considered it and run over the problems which it raises.'

The statement, that 'it is more advantageous to be governed by the best laws than by the best man', is ill formed if taken literally, because the word 'governed' has a different meaning in 'governed by a man' from what it has in 'governed by a law'. The alternatives are not exclusive; one can be, and nearly always is, governed at the same time both by a man and by laws. The exclusive alternatives are being governed by a ruler who is subject to law in his ruling and being governed by a ruler who is not subject to law but may do anything he chooses. But this is almost certainly what Aristotle means; and his way of putting it is more idiomatic and gives rise to no error in this chapter.

Some connexion seems to be implied between the rule of law and the rule of a majority. We pass with strange ease from the former to the latter. Each of them is opposed to the rule of one man, and Aristotle writes as if the two oppositions were the same. Yet in Book IV he recognizes a lawless form of democracy.

At the beginning of the chapter we seem to be getting at last to the rule of law. But once again this topic submerges. Aristotle opposes the rule of the one good man to the rule of law, but he also opposes it to the rule of many good men; and in this chapter the latter opposition soon gets his attention away from the former.

He affirms that the rule of many good men is better than the rule of one good man. Thus he appears tacitly to drop the doctrine of III 13, that we should all gladly acknowledge the 'god among men' as our king if he appears, and to return to his view in III 11, that many inferior persons form a better sovereign than a few good persons.

The main argument now for this doctrine is that the large quantity is less corruptible. The species of corruption which he offers as an example here is being 'overcome by anger or some other such passion'. He does not have our contemporary tendency to equate corruption with venality, which is really one of the species of corruption. Nowadays, if a man says 'the civil service is corrupt', people think he means it is venal; but there are other and worse sorts of corruption than venality, and it was these that Acton had in mind when he wrote that 'power tends to corrupt, and absolute power corrupts absolutely'.

Another argument is that, if we choose the rule of one good man, the problem of the succession will soon bring it about that the one ruler is not a good man.

Neither of these arguments was produced in III 11; and the arguments given there are not reproduced here.

The argument which Aristotle now contemplates *against* this position is also different. Now it is that a many will have dissensions, which one man will not. In III 11 it was that only another statesman can properly judge the performance of a statesman, and that the election and audit of officers, being of the greatest moment, should not be entrusted to the ordinary man.

III 16. SUMMARY. *It is argued that the rule of law is preferable to that of any one citizen, since the law is reason without appetite, and that, while of course the officers are supreme in deciding certain matters which the law cannot determine, each officer decides well if he has been trained by the law.*

TRANSLATION. 1287ª1. Our topic now is the king who does everything according to his own pleasure; and it is he whom we must examine. The so called legal king is not a sort of constitution, as we have said; for perpetual general-ship can exist in all of them, including democracy and aristocracy; and many put one man in control of the administration. There is in fact some such office both at Epidamnus and, to a somewhat smaller extent, at Opus. But in the case of what is called total kingship (that is, when the king governs everything as he pleases), some people think it is not even natural for one man to control all the citizens, where the city consists of like persons. For, they say, those who are alike by nature must have the same natural right and worth. Hence, just as it is harmful for bodies that unequal men should have equal food or cloth-ing, so also it is with regard to honours. Similarly, for equal men to have inequality. The right thing, therefore, is to do no more ruling than being ruled, and hence rotation is right.

1287ª18. Now this means law: for order is law. The rule of law is thus preferable to that of any one citizen. And, by this same principle, even if it were better that certain persons should rule, they should be appointed guardians and servants of the laws. Some persons must be rulers;

but, they say, it is not right that it should be one man when all are alike. As to those things which the law seems unable to decide, they could not be known by a man either. And, after educating them for this very purpose, the law delegates the rest to the rulers to judge and determine as rightly as possible. Furthermore, it allows itself to be corrected in any way that is found by experience to be better than the standing laws. He therefore who bids the law to rule seems to be bidding God and reason to rule alone; but he who bids a man rule adds a beast thereto; for desire is that sort of thing, and passion distorts rulers and the best men. Hence the law is reason without appetite.

1287ᵃ33. The argument from the arts, that healing by the book is bad, and it is preferable to employ those who possess the arts, appears to be false. Physicians do not transgress principles out of friendship; they earn their reward by healing the sick. Men in political commands, on the other hand, are accustomed to do many things out of favour or insult. For that matter, men would prefer to seek treatment out of books, whenever they suspect that enemies have persuaded their physicians to destroy them for gain. But physicians when sick call in other physicians to treat them, and coaches when in training call in other coaches, as being unable to judge truly because judging in their own affairs and being in a state of emotion. So it is plain that in seeking the right they are seeking the mean; for the law is the mean.

1287ᵇ5. Again, the customary laws are more important, and concern more important things, than the written; so that a man may be a safer ruler than the written but not safer than the customary laws.

1287ᵇ8. Further, it is not easy for one man to supervise many things. Hence those appointed officers by him will need to be numerous. And what difference is there between his appointing them in this way and their existing from the beginning?

1287ᵇ11. Again, as has been said earlier, if the good man ought to rule because he is better, two good men are still better than one. This is the 'when two go together', and Agamemnon's 'would I had ten such advisers'.

1287ᵇ15. The officers do in fact have power to decide certain matters which the law cannot determine, for instance the judge. But where it can do so, there no one claims that the law would not be the best ruler and decider. Some matters can be covered by the laws and others cannot; and it is the latter which make us doubt and ask whether it is preferable for the best law or the best man to rule. To lay down laws for the matters about which men deliberate is an impossibility. They do not deny this, that the judge of such matters must be a man, but only that he must be one man and not many.

1287ᵇ25. Each officer decides well if he has been trained by the law; and it would seem rather absurd if a man saw better when judging with two eyes and two ears, and acting with two feet and hands, than many men did with many. In actual fact monarchs make themselves many eyes and ears and hands and feet, for they make colleagues of those who are friendly to the government and to themselves. If they are not friends they will not act according to the monarch's policy; but, if they are friends both of him and the government, a friend is equal and alike, and so, if he thinks they ought to rule, he thinks that the equal and alike ought to rule alike.

1287ᵇ35. These, then, are, roughly, the things said by those who dispute against kingship.

COMMENT. The whole of this chapter is an argument in favour of the rule of law, and against the rule of an absolute king. At first it demands the rule of law only among equals (1287ᵃ12): but as it goes on it brings arguments against absolute kingship that really apply to any society.

Law is here regarded as a mean (1287ᵇ4). Why is this? Perhaps because obedience to it produces a state of affairs which is between A's getting too much at the expense of B and B's getting too much at the expense of A.

Law is here regarded as natural (1287ᵃ11, 12, 13), and hence as not altogether manmade but in some way standing over against man, as man's teacher rather than his creature, as God or Reason, and as having part of its origin in custom rather than in words (1287ᵇ6).

Aristotle does not say in this chapter whether he himself holds these views. He puts the whole chapter in the form of a report on some other persons' views. Filmer, who favoured absolute kingship, was careful to point out that the chapter does not adopt these arguments against kingship but merely reports them. Those who favour constitutional government, on the contrary, tend to assume that Aristotle endorses what he here reports, and to avoid mentioning the fact that he does not here say he endorses it.

I find it remarkable that Professor Havelock made no use of this chapter in his attempt to reconstruct Greek liberalism from the reports of Aristotle in his *Politics* (Eric A. Havelock, *The Liberal Temper in Greek Politics*, c. xii). Law is in my opinion something we must have if, while enjoying the benefits of being governed, we are to remain *free* from oppression by our governors; and I therefore include in what I mean by 'liberalism' the demand that our governors shall be bound by public laws. Hence, if I were looking for reports about Greek 'liberals' in the pages of Aristotle, I should certainly include this chapter entirely devoted to reporting a demand that rulers be bound by law. Professor Havelock's use of the word 'liberalism' must be different from mine.

I think the explanation is that the conception of law implied in this chapter conflicts with the conception of it imputed by Professor Havelock to his, I fear, mythical 'liberals'. Whereas the thinkers here reported by Aristotle regard law as natural, Professor Havelock's 'liberals' are firm that law is not nature but 'human convention historically applied, [and that] there is no one unique law or set of laws, but only an unending series of arrangements and integrations, [and that] there can, strictly speaking, be no law that is not democratic law' (402).

Did Aristotle himself regard law as natural or as conventional? This question is difficult because his only word for law, which is *nomos*, also has two other meanings, namely (2) convention and (3) general opinion. Like everybody else, he opposes nomos in the sense of (3) general opinion to nature or what the facts really are. (E.g. *Nic. Eth.* 1094ᵇ16: 'The good and the right come to seem to exist merely in the general opinion, and not in nature.') Like everybody else, again, he sometimes opposes nomos in the sense of (2) convention to nature, notably in *Nic. Eth.* V 7, where he says that some of our rules of justice involve a conventional element but others are natural. As to nomos in the sense of (1) law, I think there is no place where he opposes it to nature. It is remarkable that he devotes more than a page to a discussion whether it is wise to alter the laws (in *Politics* II 8) without opposing law to nature in any way. On the other hand, I think there is also no place where he explicitly and on his own account declares law as such to be natural. The nearest he comes to this (and it is not near) is his implication that law is not analogous to art (1269ᵃ19–20).

If the question had been put to him, I think he would have replied that, while some laws are no doubt unnatural and bad, it is highly natural that law should exist and reign in the cities of men. I think he would have said that the naturalness of law follows from the naturalness of the city, which he explicitly asserts at length (in *Politics* I 2, cf. 1278ᵇ19 'by nature man is a political animal'). Even the city ruled by the 'god among men', I think he would have said, naturally exhibits a reign of law, and only the 'god' himself is exempt from it. In his *Topics* he objects to the proposition that 'the law is a measure or image of natural justice' (140ᵃ7), but only because 'measure or image' is worse than metaphorical; he probably accepted the linking of the law with natural justice. In his *Rhetoric* he affirms in his own person that there is a common law which is according to nature (1373ᵇ6, cf. 1375ᵃ32).

III 17. SUMMARY. *Yet, when one man becomes so outstanding in goodness that his goodness exceeds that of all the others, he ought to be king.*

TRANSLATION. 1287ᵇ36. Perhaps, however, things are like this in some cases but not in others. For both the right and the advantageous are by nature one thing for the despotic constitution, another for the royal, and another for the constitutional. There is none by nature for the tyrannical, nor for the other constitutions that are perversions, since they are contrary to nature. What we have said makes it clear that among similars and equals it is neither advantageous nor right for one to be in control of all, whether there are laws or no law except himself, whether he and they are both good or neither of them good, not even if he is better than they in goodness, except in one case. We must now say what this case is, although we have already said it in a way.

1288ᵃ6. First we must distinguish the royal and the aristocratic and the constitutional. A royal people is one that naturally produces a stock that excels in goodness of political leadership. An aristocratic people is one that naturally produces a stock capable of being ruled in the freemen's way by leaders in the goodness appropriate to political rule. A constitutional people is one in which there naturally arises a political stock capable of ruling and being ruled under a law that allots the offices to the prosperous according to merit.

1288ᵃ15. Now when a whole family, or even some one person, happens to become so outstanding in goodness that his goodness exceeds that of all the others, then it is right for this family to be royal and sovereign over all, and for this individual to be king. For, as was said earlier, this accords not only with justice as customarily put forward by those who establish constitutions, whether aristocratic or oligarchic or again democratic (for they all claim in virtue of some superiority, only not the same one), but also with what was said before. That is, it is obviously not fitting to kill or exile such a man, or to ostracize him, or to ask him to be ruled in turn. For it is not natural for the part to exceed the whole, but that is what has happened to a man whose superiority is of this order. There is nothing left, therefore, but for such a one to be obeyed and to be sovereign not by turns but absolutely.

1288ª30. So much for kingship, what differences it displays, and whether it is advantageous for cities or not, and for which of them, and how.

III 18. SUMMARY. *His education will be practically the same as that of the good man.*

TRANSLATION. 1288ª32. Since we say that the correct constitutions are three, and the best of them must be that which is managed by the best men, and such is that in which there is either one man exceeding all or a whole family or a multitude exceeding in goodness, the one side being capable of obeying and the other of ruling with a view to the most eligible life, and since we showed in our first discussions that the goodness of a man must be identical with that of a citizen of the best city, it is plain that the way and the means by which a man becomes good are the same as those by which one would construct an aristocratic or kingly city, and hence the education and the customs that make a man good will be practically the same as those that make him political and kingly.

1288b2. Having decided these matters, we must now try to speak about the best constitution, in what way it naturally arises and how it is established.

COMMENT (III 17–18). In these chapters Aristotle is no longer reporting the views of others but expressing his own, at first tentatively ('Perhaps, however') and then firmly ('What we have said makes it clear that'). It turns out that he is against establishing equality of political power in all places at all times. A simple undiscriminating demand for political equality everywhere now, like our contemporary simple undiscriminating demands for external independence and internal democracy everywhere now, appears to him to overlook the actual sociological differences between peoples and to be rendered unwise by them. Different sorts of peoples require different sorts of constitution. There certainly do exist peoples who are so alike and equal that equality in ruling and being ruled is best for them. He calls them 'constitutional' peoples, meaning probably that the right constitution for them is 'constitution' in the narrow sense; and he describes them as those 'in which there naturally arises a political stock capable of ruling and being ruled under a law that allots the offices to the prosperous according to merit'. I suppose he means a fairly large political stock in proportion to the population, of the same order of ratio as the voting citizens at Athens.

At the other extreme, he holds, there certainly exist 'royal' peoples, 'naturally producing a stock that excels in goodness of political leadership'. Here I suppose him to mean a very much smaller stock in proportion to the whole, perhaps a single educated family in a people of lowly peasants. In such a people, when one man becomes 'so outstanding in goodness that his goodness exceeds that of all the others', it will be just for him to be permanent king, by the same principle of justice as egalitarians appeal to.

Thus the idea which arose out of his aporetic in III 13, namely that for some societies absolute monarchy is the best constitution, is definitely adopted by him in III 17. It is not that he rejects the intervening considerations in favour of equality and the rule of law. They too have their time and place, which no doubt included Athens. What he rejects is the general principle that there is only one right constitution, the same for all peoples at all times, no matter what the peculiarities of their society and culture and circumstances. I wish he had said so here explicitly. But he says it clearly enough in the next book, particularly in IV 12.

The monarchy that he has in mind here is absolute monarchy, untrammelled by law. 'For such men as these there is no law; they themselves are law; [and] anyone who tried to legislate for them would be ridiculous' (III 13, 1284^{a}13). Two aspects of his conception of law helped him to this view. (1) Law is a moral educator according to Aristotle (e.g. 1280^{b}12); but you cannot morally educate a person who is already a perfectly good man. (2) Law is essentially an affair for equals (1284^{a}12; less clearly 1287^{a}12–18); hence inapplicable to this supremely unequal 'god among men'.

Aristotle is right that different societies require different constitutions, and that there are societies that require monarchy, or at least have been such in the past. Our world was better off in the past, when it was led by the British, who recognized this fact, than it is now when led by the Russians and the Americans, both of whom believe that all societies require the same constitution, though they do not agree as to what that constitution is.

Aristotle is wrong, however, in thinking that any society ever requires a ruler untrammelled by law. That everybody shall be subject to law, including the ruler himself, is something we must demand at all times and places, and perhaps the only universally proper political demand. Aristotle does not give due weight to the argument that power corrupts, so that the best man is unlikely to remain the best man if there is no law to control him. This argument is not among those which he reports in III 16. Yet he was aware of it, for in VI 4, 1318ᵇ40, he writes: 'It is salutary to be responsible, and not to be able to do everything one may decide on; the ability to do whatever one wishes cannot guard against the evil in every man.'

It is disappointing to find Aristotle making an exception to the rule of law, even if it is an exception that can hardly arise in practical politics. If we believe in the rule of law, we tend to look to Aristotle as the source of that doctrine, to confirm our faith. But the first recommender of a great idea often retains many older and inconsistent ideas along with it, and hence disappoints later readers when they come to him as to the fountainhead of the idea which they prize, and whose implications they grasp more clearly than its first champion did. The admirer of Kepler's description of planetary motion may easily be cast down by reading Kepler himself.

Aristotle is wrong, also, in thinking that law is for equals only. Law is essential for and between equals and unequals alike, if they are to have any peace, or at least any contented peace. It is more important that parents obey law in dealing with their children than that they obey it in dealing with another parent. It is more important that the strong obey law in dealing with the weak than that they do so in dealing with the equally strong.

There is only one small kind of equality inherent in law, namely that everyone to whom the law applies is bound by it in the way in which it applies to him, and it ought to be enforced upon him, which is what is meant by 'equality before the law'. The rule of law is consistent with inequality in every other respect. For instance, it does not require that the poor man pay an income-tax equal to that paid by the rich man.

IV 1–2. POLITICAL SCIENCE

IV 1. SUMMARY. *The science which asks (1) what is the best constitution should also ask (2) which constitution suits which cities, (3) how any given constitution can be produced and preserved, (4) which constitution most suits all cities, (5) how many sorts of constitution there are, and (6) which laws are the best and which laws fit each of the constitutions.*

TRANSLATION. 1288^b10. In every art and science that is not a part, but is the complete account of some one genus, it belongs to a single science to examine what is suitable concerning each genus. For example, which sort of training benefits which sort of body; and what is the best training (since the best must suit the best endowed and equipped body); and which one suits the greatest number of them all (for this too is a function of the art of gymnastics). And if someone wants only a lower grade of fitness either of his body or of his knowledge, insufficient for actual competition, it is no less the business of the coach and trainer to produce this capacity too. We see the same thing happening both in medicine and in shipbuilding and clothing and in every other art.

1288^b21. Hence it is clear that in the case of a constitution also it belongs to one and the same science to examine all of the following. (1) Which is the best constitution? That is, what sort of constitution would be most desirable if there were no external hindrances to its realization?

1288^b24. (2) Which constitution suits which persons? Since for many people it is perhaps impossible to achieve the best, the good legislator and the true politician must know both what is best absolutely and what is best in the circumstances.

1288ᵇ28. (3) Thirdly, the hypothetical constitution. With regard to any given constitution the political scientist ought to be capable of examining both how it could originally be produced and thereafter how it could be preserved as long as possible. I mean, for example, if a city happens to have neither the best constitution (not possessing the resources which that needs), nor the one that its circumstances permit, but a worse one.

1288ᵇ33. (4) And besides all these he should know what constitution most suits all cities. The greater part of those who discuss constitutions, even if they are good in other ways, are not as *useful* as they might be. One should consider not merely the best but also the practicable constitution, and similarly the constitution that is easier and more available to all cities. But some students of politics seek only the topmost constitution, which requires great equipment; and those who do offer something more attainable abolish the existing constitutions and praise the Spartan or some other. We should propose an arrangement that makes it easy both for people to be persuaded to adopt it and for them to be able to make the transition from their existing arrangements. It is, indeed, no less work to correct a constitution than to establish it in the beginning, just as it is no less work to unlearn something than to learn it in the beginning. Hence in addition to the abovementioned tasks the politician should also be able to help existing constitutions, as was also said earlier.

1289ᵃ7. Now this is impossible unless one knows (5) how many sorts of constitution there are. Some people think there is only one democracy and only one oligarchy; but this is not true, and therefore we ought to note the varieties of these constitutions, both how many they are, and in how many ways they are put together.

1289ᵃ11. (6) It is part of this same wisdom to see both which laws are the best and which laws fit each of the constitutions. Laws should be made to suit the constitutions, and they always are, not constitutions to suit the laws. For a constitution is an arrangement of the city in respect of the manner in which the offices are distributed, the sovereign element in the constitution, and the end of each community; whereas the laws which are separate from those defining the constitution are those according to which the officers are to govern and prevent offenders against them. Hence clearly a knowledge of the differences and of the definition of each constitution is also necessary for the making of laws. The same laws cannot suit all oligarchies or all democracies, since there are not merely one but many democracies and also oligarchies.

COMMENT. The previous book ends with 'we must now try to speak about the best constitution'. This book, however, does not speak about the best constitution, and seems to imply (in the first paragraph of its second chapter) that the best constitution has already been dealt with. In fact, Aristotle's construction of the best constitution comes at the end of his *Politics*, in Books VII–VIII. This strange incoherence has led to many editorial reorderings of the books, and they in turn have led to much confusion. It is impossible to produce, from the text which we have, an orderly sequence forming a unified whole. We must devote ourselves to learning as much as we can from the ideas as actually presented.

Aristotle regards politics as a 'science' or 'art' or 'ability' or 'philosophy' (1282ᵇ14–23) or 'wisdom' (1289ᵃ12). In his *Ethics* he also regards it as the supreme practical science or wisdom: it makes men act well, and to act well is the aim of life. Here he regards himself as introducing and recommending an important extension of the field of politics. He says in effect that this science, though intended to be practical, has not been actually useful because it has confined itself to constructing utopias, and utopias cannot be realized in ordinary cities. He proposes to add to the search for utopia five other questions, whose answers will be very much more directly useful to the practising statesman or founder of cities.

The field and nature of science, together with its division into the various sciences, is one of the topics on which Aristotle is a supreme master. The world is made up of 'kinds' or 'genera', according to him; and each of these 'genera' requires separate study, because it has principles peculiar to itself. You cannot satisfactorily explain all 'genera' from a single set of principles; to suppose that you could was the fundamental error of the Platonic dialectic. In many fields, also, the method will be different; Plato's dialectic was erroneous, again, in offering itself as a single method adequate for all studies. It follows that knowledge falls into many departments, each being the study of a single genus, and requiring separate pursuit. (In the case of politics this genus is the constitution.) Thus the contemporary English-speaking university with its many 'departments' is a thoroughly Aristotelian idea.

Of course this idea has its disadvantages and abuses. We must not blame it for the increasing estrangement of students from each other; for that seems inherent in the advance and particularization of science. But it is to blame for the secret territory-wars that go on in universities nowadays, and for the sad assumption, often found in our pupils, that no man is entitled to speak, or even to read, in more than one department.

But Aristotle would have had none of that. He himself created and wrote in several different departments. He said that science needs to be divided, but not that scientists need to be. His remarks here on the science of politics are wholly beneficent. They consist simply in pointing out new and fruitful lines of inquiry, which he then takes up in Books IV–VI. Theoretical politics now becomes for the first time, what practical politics always is, an 'art of the possible'. Aristotle regards himself as 'helping existing constitutions' (1289ª6).

This desire to help is connected with his reluctance to adopt political principles and his preference for merely reporting other people's political principles. He is a physician at heart. Rather than join in the fighting, he will tend the wounded and suggest how peace might be made.

IV 2. SUMMARY. *From best to worst the constitutions are: kingship, aristocracy, 'constitution', democracy, oligarchy, tyranny.*

Programme: (1) What are the differences in the constitutions? (2) Which is most available and desirable after the best constitution? (3) Is there an aristocratic constitution suitable for most cities? (4) Which constitutions suit which persons? (5) How should each constitution be established? (6) What things destroy or preserve the constitutions?

TRANSLATION. 1289ª26. In our first inquiry about the constitutions we distinguished three correct ones, kingship, aristocracy, and 'constitution', and their three perversions, tyranny the perversion of kingship, oligarchy that of aristocracy, and democracy that of 'constitution'. We have now spoken of aristocracy and kingship; for to examine the best constitution is the same thing as to talk about these names, since each of them assumes personal goodness and material equipment. We have also determined how aristocracy and kingship differ from each other, and when to have a kingship. It remains to deal with the constitution that is called by the common name, and with the other constitutions, oligarchy and democracy and tyranny.

1289ª38. Now it is plain with regard to these perversions also which is worst and which second. The perversion of the first and most divine must be worst; and kingship must either be kingship merely in name and not also in fact, or else depend on great superiority in the man who is reigning. Hence tyranny, being worst, is farthest removed from a constitution; oligarchy is second (aristocracy is very far from this constitution); and democracy is the most moderate. This has already been said by somebody. He, however, did not regard it in the same way as ourselves: he considered that where they are all good (for example, oligarchy good, and so on) the worst is democracy, and where they are bad it is the best. We on the contrary say that these forms are mistaken in principle, and no oligarchy should be called better than another, but merely less bad. But let us drop this sort of judgement for the present.

1289ᵇ12.(1) First we must distinguish the differences in

the constitutions, since there are several kinds both of democracy and of oligarchy. (2) Next we must ask which is most available and which is most desirable after the best constitution. (3) And if there is any other constitution which though aristocratic and well put together is at the same time suitable for most cities, what is it? (4) Further, which of the rest is desirable for which persons? For it may be that some need democracy rather than oligarchy, but others the latter rather than the former. (5) Next, how should a man establish these constitutions when he wishes to do so, that is to say, democracies of each form and again oligarchies? (6) Finally, when we have succinctly rehearsed all these matters as far as possible, we must try to investigate what things destroy or preserve the constitutions, both generally and in particular, and what are the most natural causes of these things.

COMMENT. Aristotle puts his six constitutions in an order of merit, and remarks that 'this has already been said by somebody'. This reminds Platonists of a passage in Plato's *Statesman* (302–3). But that passage does not in fact differ from Aristotle in the detail mentioned by Aristotle. On the contrary, Plato there, just like Aristotle here, regards oligarchy as never being a good form. Perhaps Aristotle when writing this did not remember where he got it, and also slightly misremembered it to his own advantage, as the human mind is prone to do. The *Statesman* is a dialogue that Aristotle never refers to by title or author.

We have here a second list of the questions of politics. It corresponds very imperfectly with the list in the previous chapter. And neither of the two lists corresponds closely with what Aristotle actually does in the rest of the book.

IV 3–7. SUBDIVISIONS OF THE
CONSTITUTIONS

IV 3. SUMMARY. *Every city has more than one part. Of these parts sometimes all participate in the government, sometimes a minority, sometimes a majority. This inevitably makes a plurality of kinds of constitution, and not just two as commonly thought.*

TRANSLATION. 1289ᵇ27. The cause of there being more than one constitution is that every city has more than one part. In the first place, we see that all cities are composed of families. Next, of this population some must be prosperous, others needy, and others intermediate, the prosperous owning arms but the needy not. And we see that the demos is sometimes agricultural, sometimes mercantile, and sometimes working-class. The notables also differ among themselves both in wealth and in the extent of their property. Keeping horses, for example, is a difficult thing to do unless one is rich. That is why in ancient times every city whose power lay in its horses was an oligarchy. Peoples such as the Eretrians, the Chalcidians, the Magnesians on the Meander, and many others in Asia, used horses against their neighbours in their wars. In addition to differences in wealth there are differences in birth and in personal goodness. To these must be added any other part of a city that was mentioned in the discussion of aristocracy, where we distinguished what parts are essential to every city.

1290ᵃ3. Of these parts sometimes all participate in the government, sometimes a minority, sometimes a majority. It is therefore plain that there must be a plurality of constitutions differing from each other in kind, since these parts of which they are composed differ in kind. For a constitution is an arrangement of the offices; and offices are always distributed either in accordance with the power of the participators, or in accordance with some equality which is common to them, I mean, for example, the equality of the needy as such, or that of the prosperous, or something common to both. There must therefore be as many constitutions as there are arrangements in respect of the ratios and differences of the parts.

1290ª13. They are usually thought to be two. Just as the winds are called either north or south, and the rest perversions of those, so there are thought to be two constitutions, demos and oligarchy. Aristocracy is reckoned a kind of oligarchy, as being oligarchy of a sort; and the so called 'constitution' is reckoned a kind of democracy, just as they reckon the west wind a norther and the east wind a souther. The same thing happens with scales, according to some: there also they make two kinds, the Dorian and the Phrygian; and they call the other modes either 'Doric' or 'Phrygic'. Usually men are accustomed to think about constitutions too in this way; but it is truer and better to follow our division: the well-formed constitution is of one or two kinds only, and the others are perversions of it, either of the well-mixed harmony or of the best constitution, the more taut and despotic being oligarchic, the slack and soft demotic.

IV 4. SUMMARY. *Democracy is when the free and needy, being in a majority, are in control of the government. It varies according to the class of person predominating. The first kind is the 'equal' kind, that is, where neither the needy nor the prosperous have any ascendancy, but they are both alike. There are three intermediate kinds. The fifth and last is where the mass is sovereign and not the law. Here demagogues arise.*

TRANSLATION. 1290ª30. Democracy should not be taken

simply as the constitution where the majority is in control, although some people habitually take it so nowadays; for the larger part is in control in oligarchies too, and everywhere. Nor should oligarchy be taken as where a few are in control of the State. If out of a total of thirteen hundred a thousand were rich, and these rich did not share office with the three hundred poor although the latter were free and similar to them in other respects, no one would say these people had a democracy. Similarly, if there were only a few poor men, but they were stronger than the prosperous majority, no one would call such a constitution an oligarchy, if the rich did not participate in the honours. It is therefore better to say that there is a demos when the free are in power, and an oligarchy when the rich are, but the former happen to be many and the latter happen to be few, since many are free, but few are rich. Otherwise there would be an oligarchy if the offices were distributed according to height, as is said to happen in Ethiopia, or according to beauty, since the handsome and the tall are both few in number.

1290^{b}7. However, to define these constitutions by these marks alone is still not sufficient. Since both the demos and the oligarchy have more than one part, we must distinguish them further as follows: it is not a demos if the free are few and rule over a majority that is not free, as in Apollonia on the Ionian Gulf and in Thera. In each of these cities the honours belonged to those who stood out in birth and had first occupied the colony, and they were few among many. Nor is it an oligarchy if the rich rule because they are in the majority, as formerly in Colophon, where the majority had acquired substantial property before the war against the Lydians. It is a democracy when the free and needy, being in a majority, are in control of the government, and an oligarchy when the rich and better born, who are few, are so.

1290ᵇ21. We have said that there is more than one constitution, and for what cause. Let us now say that there are more than we have said, and what they are, and why. Let us begin from our previous agreement that every city has not one but several parts.

1290ᵇ25. If we were going to classify kinds of animal, we should first distinguish what it is necessary for every animal to have. For example, it must have some of the sense-organs, and something like a mouth and stomach to work and receive the food. Besides these it must have parts by which it moves. If these were all there were, and they had differences (I mean for example that there were several kinds of mouth and stomach and sense-organ, and also of the locomotive parts), then the number of the combination of these must produce several sorts of animal, since it is impossible for the same animal to have several kinds of mouth, or of ear. Hence when all the possible couplings of these differences are taken, they will make kinds of animal, and as many kinds of animal as there are combinations of the necessary parts.

1290ᵇ37. It is the same with the constitutions we have mentioned. Cities also consist not of one but of many parts, as has often been mentioned. (1) One of these parts is the class concerned with food, called farmers.

(2) A second is what is called the working class. This is the class concerned with the crafts without which a city cannot be inhabited, some of which are necessary, while others are for luxury or fine living.

(3) A third is the marketeering class, where by 'marketeering' I mean the class occupied in sales and purchases and trade and retail.

(4) A fourth is the hired men.

(5) A fifth sort is the defenders, who are no less necessary than the foregoing if the citizens are not to become the slaves of invaders. (And it is surely impossible that anything should deserve the name of 'city' if it is slavish in nature. A city is selfsufficient; but a slave is not selfsufficient.)

1291ª10. It follows that the passage in the *Republic* though elegant is inadequate. 'Socrates' there says that the most necessary parts of a city are four, namely a weaver, a farmer, a shoemaker, and a housebuilder. Later, considering these not selfsufficient, he adds a smith and those concerned with the necessary livestock, and further a merchant and a retailer; and these together make up the complement of the first city. The implication is that every city exists for the sake of necessities, and not rather for the sake of the noble, and that it has equal need of shoemakers and farmers. He does not provide the defending part until they have got into war by extending their land and seizing some of the neighbours'. However, even among the four and whatever associates they have there must be someone to judge and render justice. If now one would also reckon the mind as part of an animal, and more so than the body, then one should also reckon as parts of cities, and more so than those directed to necessary use, such parts as these, namely the fighters, those who handle forensic justice, and besides them the deliberators, deliberating being a function of political intelligence. Nor does it make any difference to the argument whether they are embodied in distinct persons or in the same persons. Fighting and farming are often found in the same persons too. Since, therefore, both the latter and the former are to be reckoned parts of the city, the soldiery is evidently a necessary part of the city.

(7) Seventh are those who serve with their property. These we call the prosperous.

(8) Eighth is the class of public servants, those who serve in connexion with the offices, since there cannot be a city without officers. There must therefore be persons who can govern and serve the city in that way, either continuously or in turn.

1291ᵃ38. There remain those we have just distinguished, who deliberate and judge disputes about justice. Since these ought to be present in cities, and be present in a good and just form, there must also be some citizens who possess some personal goodness.

1291ᵇ2. Many men think that men can possess most of these capacities jointly with others, being for example both defenders and farmers and craftsmen, or both deliberators and judges; and all men claim to possess goodness too, and think they can fill most offices. But no one can be both poor and rich. Hence these seem to be especially parts of a city, the prosperous and the needy. Also the fact that usually the former are few and the latter many makes them appear opposites among the city's parts. That is why people set up the constitutions according to which of these parts is dominant, and it comes to be thought that constitutions are two, democracy and oligarchy.

1291ᵇ14. We have said that there is more than one constitution, and for what causes. Let us now say that there is also more than one kind of democracy and of oligarchy. This is clear from what has already been said. There is more than one kind of demos, and of the so called notables. Thus one kind of demos is the farmers; another the persons concerned with crafts; another the marketeering, concerned with purchase and sale; another the maritime, and this is part naval, part commercial, part transport, part fishery. Each of these is numerous in many places, for example fishermen at Tarentum and Byzantium, navy men at Athens, traders at Aegina and Chios, transporters at Tenedos. Besides these there are the manual labourers and those who have too little property to be able to take time off. Also those who are free by one parent only, and any other such kind of class. The notables subdivide by wealth, birth, goodness, education, and the other qualities that are ascribed on the same principle.

1291ᵇ30. (1) The first kind of democracy is that which is so called mainly with respect to equality. By 'equality' is meant, in the law of this kind of democracy, that neither the needy nor the prosperous have any ascendancy, and neither are in power, but they are both alike. If freedom and equality exist most in democracy, as some people believe, that would be most so when everyone most shares alike in the constitution. The demos being a majority, and the opinion of the majority being sovereign, this must be a democracy. This then is one sort of democracy.

1291ᵇ39. (2) Another is where the offices require property qualifications, and these are low; every man who acquires them must have the right to share, and must lose it when he loses them.

1292ᵃ1. (3) Another kind of democracy is where all the citizens participate who are unchallenged, and the law rules.

1292ᵃ2. (4) Another kind of democracy is where everyone participates in the offices merely by being a citizen, and the law rules.

1292ᵃ4. (5) Another kind of democracy is where other matters are the same, but the mass is sovereign and not the law. This kind arises when decrees are sovereign instead of the law; and this happens because of the demagogues. In lawabiding democracies the demagogue does not arise; on the contrary, the best of the citizens preside. But where the laws are not sovereign, there demagogues arise. This is because the demos becomes a monarch, one person composed of many; for the many are sovereign not as individuals but all together.

1292ᵃ13. When Homer says that to have many chiefs is not good, it is obscure whether he means this kind of constitution, or that where there are several individual rulers. Anyhow, this kind of demos, not being ruled by law, seeks to act like the sole ruler that it is. It becomes despotic; and flatterers are held in honour. Such a demos is the analogue of tyranny among the monarchies. They both have the same character. They are both despotic towards the better persons. The decrees of the one are like the edicts of the other. The demagogue and the flatterer are the same and analogous. Each attain their greatest power with each, the flatterers with the tyrants and the demagogues with this kind of demos. It is they who, by referring everything to the demos, cause decrees to be sovereign instead of laws. For they grow great through the demos being sovereign over everything and their being sovereign over the opinion of the demos, because the mass believes them. Furthermore, persons who are accusing the governors say that the demos ought to decide; the demos gladly accepts the challenge; and so the whole government is undermined.

1292ᵃ30. It would seem reasonable to object that this kind of democracy is not a constitution at all, on the ground that where laws do not rule there is no constitution. The law should rule over all general matters, the officers over particulars; and that should be considered a constitution. It clearly follows that, if democracy is one of the

constitutions, such a state of affairs as this, in which everything is settled by decrees, is not really a democracy at all,
since no decree can be general. So much for the kinds of
democracy.

COMMENT. An astonishingly unmethodical chapter. Aristotle first
considers how to define democracy, a topic which he has already
considered in III 7–8. He then proposes a general method for sub-
dividing constitutions. The method is explained by a remarkable
biological analogy: there is (we may suppose?) a certain number of
parts which any animal must have, and a certain number of forms
which each of these parts can take; hence, if we take all the possible
combinations of these forms of these parts, we shall have all the (possible? actual?) kinds of animal. Aristotle, the great empirical describer
of species, seems here to suggest that he might have arrived at his
species without any observation of animals, by pure logical division.
Next he starts to follow this method by listing the parts of a city.
This leads him to consider Plato's attempt to do the same in the
Republic, a digression which causes him to fail to number his own
sixth part, and to leave some doubt what exactly it contained. After
mysteriously referring to the parts as 'capacities' (1291^{b}2), more than
one of which may belong to the same person, he talks as if he had
included the prosperous and the needy in his list of parts (1291^{b}8),
which he has not done, at least not under those names. He then gives
a list of possible kinds of demos, which does not correspond with the
previous list of parts of a city. Lastly he distinguishes five kinds of
democracy, but without explicitly making use of either of his lists in
doing so.
The division of democracy is very brief and obscure. We can probably supply that the first two kinds are lawabiding, though he does not
tell us so; but we cannot see any clear difference between the first,
third, and fourth, forms; and the second, third, and fourth, forms
seem to be much less real than the first and last.
In spite of this exasperating unmethodicalness, the chapter is
interesting for its keen sociological observation, which recalls the
eighth book of Plato's *Republic*.
Here for the first time Aristotle raises the notion of freedom in
connexion with the definition of democracy. He reports, both here
(1291^{b}35) and elsewhere (VI 2), that democrats claim that democracy gives more freedom than any other constitution. He probably

disbelieved this himself; but he is not concerned to say so. He is concerned to say that democracy cannot be defined by freedom alone: the word does not mean just the constitution where the free are sovereign (1290ᵇ1); it means something much narrower, namely the constitution where those who are both free and needy form a majority which is sovereign (1290ᵇ18). (He comes close to equating freedom with need in 1294ᵃ10–20.)

The first kind of democracy in this chapter is 'so called mainly with respect to equality' (1291ᵇ30–39). But this kind disappears in the subsequent chapters and is not mentioned again. Hereafter Aristotle recognizes only the other four kinds of democracy. These four other kinds have nothing about equality in their description. In this respect they agree better with his discussions of the general definition of democracy (III 7–8 and IV 4, 1290ᵃ30–ᵇ20); for in them too there is nothing about equality. Thus equality is not prominent in Aristotle's conception of democracy.

The reason for this almost total absence of equality from Aristotle's conception of democracy is probably that he takes democracy literally as the sovereignty of a demos, and a demos though large is not the whole population equally. It is another side of the fact that Aristotle's democracy is the eastern dictatorship of the proletariat rather than the western equal sharing of everybody in the government.

It is probable, however, that somebody in ancient Greece had the western idea of democracy as the equal sharing by everybody in the government, or Aristotle would not have mentioned this kind of democracy even once. Somebody was moving towards the idea of government neither by a one, nor by a few, nor by a majority however large, but by the whole—and was misusing language to express himself, as original thinkers are often obliged to do.

It is difficult to see how Aristotle's second form of democracy is really a democracy in any sense. Essential to his definitions of democracy is that the sovereigns are poor; but in his second species 'the offices require property qualifications' (1291ᵇ39). These qualifications are said to be low; but, if they exist at all, they must exclude some of the poor. Does he mean only the high offices? Apparently not, because in IV 6, in describing what seems intended to be the same kind of democracy, he says that the sovereigns 'possess a moderate amount of property' (1292ᵇ26). It appears that, to be part of the sovereign in this kind of democracy, you must be poor but not too poor!

What made it possible for Aristotle to regard such a constitution as a democracy is, probably, the fact that every Greek demos that ever wielded power did have beneath itself a very large body of persons excluded from political activity, notably the slaves and the freedmen and foreigners who could not become citizens. Since this mass existed in any case, to increase it a little by requiring a low property-qualification was not felt as necessarily ending the democracy. As W. L. Newman put it in his excellent discussion of Aristotle on democracy (*The Politics of Aristotle* IV xxxvi–lxi): 'the poorer class of citizens in a Greek democracy was itself a privileged class and had classes beneath it on which it looked down.'

IV 5. SUMMARY. *There are four kinds of oligarchy. Sometimes the constitution is oligarchic but politics are conducted democratically, or conversely.*

TRANSLATION. 1292ᵃ39. One kind of oligarchy is where offices require a property-qualification high enough to exclude the needy majority, but anyone who meets it may share in the government. Another is when offices require a high property-qualification and the officers themselves make the appointments. (If they do so from all who have the qualification, that seems more like aristocracy; but if from certain specified persons, it is oligarchic.) Another kind of oligarchy is when a son succeeds his father. A fourth is when both the above happens and the officers rule instead of the law. This is the counterpart among oligarchies of tyranny among monarchies and the last-mentioned democracy among democracies; in fact they call this kind of oligarchy dynasty.

1292ᵇ11. Such are the kinds of oligarchy and democracy. We must notice, however, that it has often happened that, although the legal constitution is not democratic, custom and training cause politics to be democratically conducted. Conversely, in other places the legal constitution is more democratic, but owing to their training and customs they behave rather as an oligarchy. This happens particularly after a change of constitution. They do not go forward immediately; at first they are content to encroach little on each other. Thus the pre-existing laws continue, although the power is in the hands of those who have changed the constitution.

IV 6. SUMMARY. *There are four kinds of democracy and four kinds of oligarchy.*

TRANSLATION. 1292^b22. That there are so many kinds of democracy and oligarchy is plain from what has already been said. Either all the above-mentioned parts of the demos must take part in the government, or only some of them. When the government is in the power of the part which farms and the part which possesses a moderate amount of property, they govern in accordance with laws. They have enough to live on if they work, but they cannot take time off; so they set up the law and hold only the essential assemblies. Other people have the right to take part as soon as they acquire the assessment determined by the laws. Thus all who have acquired it have the right to take part. That some should not have the right under any circumstances is oligarchic; but it is not oligarchic to have the right but be unable to take the time because there are no revenues. This then is one kind of democracy, arising from these causes.

1292^b34. Another kind arises from the next division. The right may belong to all whose birth is unexceptionable, while only those who can take time off actually participate. Hence in such a democracy the laws govern, because there is no revenue. A third kind is where every free man has the right to share in the government, but they do not all do so for the above-mentioned cause, owing to which law necessarily rules in this kind also. A fourth kind of democracy is that which has arisen latest in time in the cities. Since cities have become much larger than they were in the beginning, and revenues are abundant, all persons have a right to participate in the government because the populace preponderates, and they do take part and govern because even the needy can take time off by getting paid for it. In fact, such a populace takes more time off than anyone else. The care of their private affairs does not hinder them at all, whereas it does hinder the rich, who consequently often do not take part in the assembly or the courts. Thus the State comes to be controlled by the populace of needy persons, and not by the laws.

1293ᵃ10. Such in number and nature are the kinds of democracy, owing to these necessities. And here are those of oligarchy. When a number of persons own property, but it is small and not too much, that is the first kind of oligarchy. They give the right to take part to everyone who has the property; and the quantity of those taking part in the government necessitates that not the men but the law is sovereign. The farther they are from monarchy, having neither so much property as to neglect it and take time off, nor so little as to be supported by the city, they necessarily expect the law to rule for them, not themselves. If, however, those who own the properties are fewer than those who formerly did so, and they own more, the second kind of oligarchy arises. Being stronger, they expect to have more; so they themselves choose who out of the rest is to join the government. But as they are not yet strong enough to rule without law they make a law to this effect. If the process of fewer persons holding larger properties intensifies, there comes the third stage of oligarchy, where they keep the offices to themselves, but this is in accordance with a law requiring dead men's places to be filled by their sons. When, finally, their excess of possessions and influence is great, such a dynasty is near to monarchy, and the men become supreme instead of the law. And this is the fourth kind of oligarchy, corresponding to the last kind of democracy.

COMMENT. The four kinds of democracy distinguished in this chapter are probably those of IV 4 minus the first. We learn more about them here than we did there. We learn that the first (which is the second of IV 4) is 'when the government is in the power of the part which farms and the part which possesses a moderate amount of property' (1292ᵇ25). Thus Aristotle now connects one of his kinds of democracy with one of the kinds of demos which he distinguished in IV 4 (1291ᵇ18), and also with one of the parts of a city distinguished there (1290ᵇ40). It is evident that Aristotle considers this the least un-desirable form of democracy, both from what he says here, and from a longer discussion in a later chapter (VI 4). The reason for his preference is that farmers, not having the leisure to attend frequent assemblies, set up the law to govern in their absence and allow it to take its course. Aristotle believes he has observed that the demos will not let law rule if it has the leisure to rule itself. He recommends democracies to make laws controlling the ownership of land so as to maintain a demos of this kind (in VI 4). The next best sort of demos consists of herdsmen. Aristotle distinguishes herdsmen from 'farmers' or tillers; but a city controlled by a demos of herdsmen still ranks in his eyes as a democracy of the first and best kind (1319ᵃ39).

The second and third kinds of democracy in IV 6 are as shadowy as they were in IV 4 (where they were numbered third and fourth). They are not connected with any special kind of demos, either here or in their final appearance in VI 4 (1319ᵃ40). But Aristotle says in IV 12 that each kind of democracy is adapted to a city where each demos preponderates (1296ᵇ27), and he there connects the first kind with a preponderance of farmers and the last with a preponderance of 'workmen and wage-earners'. Workmen and wage-earners were not included among the kinds of demos listed in IV 4, at least under those names; but workmen were included among the parts of a city listed there.

IV 7. SUMMARY. *The only aristocracy rightly so called is the constitution consisting of the best men absolutely; but in a looser sense there are three more.*

TRANSLATION. 1293ᵃ35. There are two more constitutions besides democracy and oligarchy. One of these is recognized by everybody and listed as one of the four constitutions, the four constitutions being monarchy, oligarchy, democracy, and fourthly what is called aristocracy. A fifth is that which is referred to by the name common to all (for they call it 'constitution'). Owing to its infrequency it escapes the notice of persons trying to count the kinds of constitution, and they use only the four in their *Constitutions* (e.g. Plato).

1293^{b}1. The name 'aristocracy' applies properly to the constitution considered in our first discussions; that is, the only aristocracy rightly so called is the constitution consisting of the best men absolutely, not of men good on some assumption. There only are the good man and the good citizen absolutely the same; elsewhere the good are good relatively to their own constitution. There are, however, some so-called aristocracies which differ both from the oligarchic and from the so-called 'constitution'. The constitution where officers are chosen not merely for their wealth, but also for their goodness, differs from both of those and is called aristocratic. For, even where there is no public concern for goodness, there are, nevertheless, persons who are well thought of and considered to be good men. Where, therefore, the constitution looks both to wealth and to goodness and to demos, as at Carthage, it is aristocratic. So it is where it looks only to the two, goodness and demos, as does that of the Spartans, and is a mixture of these two, democracy and goodness. Thus aristocracy has these two forms in addition to the first and best constitution; and thirdly there are such forms of the so-called 'constitution' as lean more towards oligarchy.

IV 8–13. WHICH CONSTITUTION MOST SUITS MOST CITIES?

IV 8. SUMMARY. *'Constitution' is in general a mixture of oligarchy and democracy, or of the prosperous and the needy, differing from aristocracy in that the good are not included as such.*

TRANSLATION. 1293ᵇ22. It remains for us to discuss the so-called 'constitution' and tyranny. We have put them in this order, although 'constitution' is not a perversion nor are the aristocracies just mentioned, because in truth they all fall short of the most correct constitution and hence are counted as perversions, while there exist perversions of them, namely those we mentioned in the beginning. To deal with tyranny last is reasonable because it is the least constitutional of all, and we are studying constitutionality. That is why matters have been arranged in this way.

1293ᵇ31. We must now set out the nature of a 'constitution'. Its force is plainer now that we have determined the facts concerning oligarchy and democracy. The 'constitution' is, to put it simply, a mixture of oligarchy and democracy. But people are accustomed to call 'constitutions' only those mixtures which incline towards democracy; those which incline rather towards oligarchy they call aristocracies, because education and breeding are commoner among the more prosperous. Further, the prosperous appear to possess that for the sake of which wrongdoers do wrong, which is why they call them both good men and notables. Since therefore aristocracy means giving the preponderance to the best of the citizens, people say of oligarchies also that they are drawn rather from the good men.

1293^{b}42. It seems impossible that a city should be well conducted if it is not ruled aristocratically, that is by the best men, but by bad men, and equally impossible that it should be ruled aristocratically if it is not well conducted. But good laws do not make a well-conducted city if they are not obeyed. We must hold, therefore, that there are two kinds of wellconductedness, one being that the standing laws are obeyed, and the other being that the laws by which they abide are good. (For bad laws can also be obeyed.) 'Good laws' here can mean either the best laws possible for them or the best absolutely.

1294^{a}9. Aristocracy is thought to consist mainly in the honours being allotted according to goodness. The mark of aristocracy is goodness, of oligarchy wealth, of demos freedom. The principle of majority rule obtains in all of them. That is, both in oligarchy and in aristocracy and in democracies, what the majority of those participating in the government decides is what prevails. Now in most cities the form of the constitution is wrongly named, because the mixture aims merely at the prosperous and needy, wealth and freedom. That is because in most of them the prosperous seem practically to take the place of the good. But since in fact there are *three* claimants to political equality, namely freedom, wealth, *and goodness* (the breeding which they cite as a fourth is a consequence of the latter two; breeding is ancient wealth and goodness), it is clear that the mixture of the two, the prosperous and the needy, should be called 'constitutional' government, and the mixture of the three should be called aristocracy— it deserves this name most of them all except the true and first one.

1294^{a}25. We have now said that there are other kinds of constitution besides monarchy and democracy and oligarchy, and what they are, and how the aristocracies and the 'constitutions' differ from each other. That they are not far from each other is plain.[1]

COMMENT. In the original definitions of the six constitutions we were told that 'constitution' in the specific sense is the constitution where the majority governs for the common advantage (III 7, 1279ᵃ37). The scheme there implied that the number of persons 'sharing in the constitution' is no smaller in 'constitution' than in democracy.

What is the definition of 'constitution' in Book IV? The answer is obscure and uncertain; but clearly it is no longer the definition of III 7. Nothing more is said about government either by a majority or in the common advantage; and there is a tendency to imply that those 'sharing in the constitution' are fewer in 'constitution' than they are in democracy.

In IV 8 we learn that ' "constitution" is, to put it simply, a mixture of oligarchy and democracy' (1293ᵇ34). This shows at once that Aristotle has abandoned the scheme of III 7; for in terms of that he would be saying that a mixture of two bad constitutions with bad aims could produce one good constitution with a good aim.

'Constitution' in the narrow sense is, then, a mixed constitution in the broad sense. Newman wrote that 'Aristotle nowhere uses the exact phrase "mixed constitutions" '; but I think that is one of Newman's rare mistakes (IV xvii n.). Aristotle has the phrase 'mixed constitution' in the next chapter (1294ᵇ35), where the word 'constitution' must have its broad sense, or 'mixed' would be as otiose as 'male' in 'male man'. Elsewhere he writes that 'some say that the best constitution should be mixed from all the constitutions' (1265ᵇ34).

What is a mixture of constitutions? The phrase is more familiar than clear. It warms our hearts because it suggests a reconciliation of our opposed parties and an end of our strife. But it has no literal meaning. You cannot mix democracy and oligarchy like gin and vermouth in a glass. In a cocktail gin and vermouth are both actually present. In a mixture of democracy and oligarchy neither is present. We might guess that a mixture of oligarchy and democracy would be where those 'sharing in the constitution' were more than in oligarchy but fewer than in democracy. But Aristotle does not at once explain. Instead he speaks of aristocracies and wellconductedness, apparently for the following reason.

[1] Eliminating τῆς ἀριστοκρατίας from line 28. It gives a meaningless sentence unless we take ἀλλήλων αἵ τ᾽ as equivalent to ἀλλήλων θ᾽ αἵ.

Various different mixtures of oligarchy and democracy are possible, some inclining more towards the one and some more towards the other. Most people do not recognize as 'constitutions' those mixtures which incline more towards oligarchy, but think of them as aristocracies. It may be hard to see why a near oligarchy should appear to be an aristocracy, but riches tend to produce goodness. A real aristocracy must really have good men and be well conducted, for aristocracy is where the honours are allotted in accordance with goodness. Aristocracy takes account of goodness as well as of riches and of free birth in allotting political honours. 'Constitution', on the other hand, takes account only of the two, riches and poverty. That is the difference between these closely resembling forms (1294ᵃ29).

Thus the chapter does not bring much clarification of its statement that 'constitution' is a mixture of oligarchy and democracy. It only tells us that some 'constitutions' deceptively resemble aristocracy, and that 'constitution' may also be described as a mixture of the prosperous and the needy. Perhaps we may infer that in 'constitution' a man obtains some eligibility for political office merely by being free, even if he is poor, but he obtains more eligibility, or eligibility to higher office, by being rich as well as free.

IV 9. SUMMARY. *This mixture may be achieved by (1) combining the legislation of oligarchy and democracy, or (2) taking the middle between them, or (3) taking some laws from each. The result should appear to be both and neither.*

TRANSLATION. 1294ᵃ30. In continuation let us next say how the so-called 'constitution' arises in distinction from democracy and oligarchy, and how it should be established. This will make plain at the same time the defining marks of democracy and oligarchy, since we must grasp the difference between these two, and then put 'constitution' together by taking as it were a tally from each of them.

1294ᵃ35. There are three marks of combination and mixture. (1) Either one should take the legislation of both constitutions, as in the matter of the lawcourts, for example, where oligarchies fine the prosperous for not attending and do not pay the needy, whereas democracies pay the needy and do not fine the prosperous. The common element and middle of these is to do both these things. That then is the 'constitutional' thing to do, being a mixture of both. This is one mode of coupling.

(2) Another way is to take the middle between what they both ordain. Thus to sit in the Assembly no assessment or a very small one is required by the one side, but a great assessment by the other. The joint thing is to require neither of these, but the middle assessment.

(3) A third is, given two sets of ordinances, to take some from the oligarchic law and some from the democratic. I mean, for example, it is thought democratic to appoint officers by lot and oligarchic to do it by election. It is also thought democratic not to require an assessment, and oligarchic to require one. It is aristocratic and 'constitutional', therefore, to take one from each, making the officers elected as in oligarchy but without assessment as in democracy. Such is the mode of mixture.

1294^{b}14. It is a mark that democracy and oligarchy have been well mixed when one can call the same constitution both a democracy and an oligarchy, since clearly what makes people talk so is that the mixing has been good. The middle too has this character: each of the extremes is discernible in it. This happens in regard to the Spartan constitution. Many people try to speak of it as a democracy because it has many democratic elements in its organization. One example is the way the children are brought up: those of the rich are brought up like those of the poor, and they are educated in a way that even the children of the poor could afford. Similarly in the next period, and when they become men, things are the same. There is nothing here to distinguish the rich from the poor. Food is the same for all at the common tables; and the clothing of the rich is such as any poor man could also provide. Another democratic element is that of the two greatest offices the people choose the one and share in the other, since they choose the Elders and share in the Overseership. Others call it an oligarchy because it has many oligarchic elements. For example, all the officers are appointed by vote and none by lot, and death and exile are imposed by a small body, and there are many other such features.

1294^{b}34. The well-mixed constitution should appear to be both and neither. It should survive by its own nature and not through outside support; and this 'by its own nature' should consist not merely in a majority's so wishing, since that could happen in a bad constitution too, but in none whatever of the city's parts in any way wishing for another constitution. We have now said how to establish a 'constitution', and likewise the so-called aristocracies.

COMMENT. This chapter gives some explanation of the metaphor of mixture. A constitution is a mixture of two others if either (1) it has whatever laws either of them has, or (2) it has a law intermediate between their corresponding laws, or (3) it has some of the laws of each of them.

The first principle would mean that the mixture necessarily had more laws than its constituents; but Aristotle does not say so. The second principle can be applied only where there is some recognizable scale of degrees, such as the amount of property that entitles a man to attend the Assembly; but Aristotle does not say so. Nor does he say whether these principles are to be applied to all the laws to which they can be applied, or to some class of laws; but almost certainly he was thinking of the laws which define the officers of the city, their number and nature and power and tenure and method of appointment; for 'the constitution is the government' in his opinion (1278^{b}11).

He seems not to be describing actual constitutions which he has observed, although that is what he is doing in his accounts of democracy, oligarchy, aristocracy, and tyranny, in this book. He seems rather to be making a proposal, or advising us how to proceed if we are ever called on to improve one of the democracies or oligarchies that abound in Greece. Thus in the first sentence, where he says he will ask how 'constitution' arises, this 'arises' is at once interpreted as being how it '*should be*' established. In the second sentence 'constitution' has to be 'put together', as if it were something to be invented. The first principle of mixture is introduced by 'Either one *should* take'. He twice tells us how to know when the constitution has been 'well' mixed (1294^{b}14, 35). His attitude towards 'constitution' is evaluative here, not descriptive as it is towards the other five constitutions in this book; and that is probably why he does not subdivide it into species.

He does mention one actual constitution in this chapter, that of Sparta. But the value-words continue through the discussion of Sparta, which therefore appears to be offered as an example of a *good* 'constitution' rather than merely of a 'constitution'. And he does not actually say that Sparta is either a 'constitution' in the narrow sense, or a mixture, either here or in his long discussion of it in Book II, chapter 9, of the *Politics*. In another part of Book II he seems to imply that Sparta was an aristocracy, and to contrast it as such with the 'constitution' in Plato's *Laws* (1265^{b}26–41). On the whole we receive from this chapter the impression that 'constitution' is something to be hoped for and realized if possible, rather than something actually there to be observed and analysed.

IV 10. SUMMARY. *There are three kinds of tyranny.*

TRANSLATION. 1295^{a}1. It remains for us to speak of tyranny, not that there is a great deal to say about it, but in order that it may take its part in the inquiry, since we put it too among the constitutions. We dealt with kingship in our first discussions, where we examined, in regard to the kind of kingship that is most commonly so called, whether it is a disadvantage or an advantage to cities, and who should be made such a king, and whence, and how. In the course of considering kingship we distinguished two kinds of tyranny, because their nature overlapped in a way with kingship too, owing to their both being legal. Some of the barbarians elect monarchs with absolute powers; and there were formerly some monarchs of this sort among the ancient Greeks, called *aesymnetes*. They differ somewhat among themselves; but they were kingly in being legal and ruling over willing subjects, and tyrannical in ruling despotically according to their own judgement. A third form of tyranny is what is considered to be tyranny in the fullest sense, and that is the counterpart of total kingship. To this class of tyranny necessarily belongs the monarchy that rules irresponsibly over all equals and betters for its own benefit, not for that of the subjects. It is therefore contrary to the will of the subjects, since no free man endures such rule if he can help it. These are the kinds of tyranny, and this is the number of them, for the reasons stated.

IV II. SUMMARY. *The happy life is the unimpeded life of goodness. Goodness is a mean. The middle in cities is the class of persons who are neither very prosperous nor very needy. They are the most fortunate, reasonable, and stable, class in the city. They ought to be numerous, and they ought to be in control. But they rarely are numerous, and so the middle constitution rarely occurs.*

TRANSLATION. 1295ᵃ25. What is the best constitution, and what is the best life, for most cities and most men, judging by the standard not of a goodness surpassing ordinary men, nor of an education requiring a fortunate nature and circumstances, nor of an ideal constitution, but of a life that the majority can live in common and a constitution that most cities can share? The so-called aristocracies that we have just been discussing either fall outside the reach of most cities or border on what is called 'constitution' (which is why they have to be treated together as one).

1295ᵃ34. All these matters are to be judged on the same principles. If it is true, as was said in the *Ethics*, that the happy life is the unimpeded life of goodness, and that goodness is a mean, then the middle life must be the best, that of the mean which it is possible for each to achieve. These same marks must apply to the goodness and badness of a city and a constitution, since the constitution is a form of the life of a city.

1295ᵇ1. Now in all cities the city has three parts, the very prosperous, the very needy, and the third class of those in the middle. Hence, since it is admitted that the moderate and middle is the best, it is clear that the gifts of fortune too are best of all when owned in a middle amount. For that makes it easiest to obey reason, whereas excessive beauty or strength or birth or wealth, or their opposites, excessive poverty or weakness or great inferiority, make it hard to follow reason. Persons of the former sort tend more to become insolent and greatly bad; the latter tend too much to become rogues and pettily bad; and crimes are done either out of insolence or out of roguery. Furthermore, the middle classes are least inclined to shun office or pursue it, and these are both harmful to cities.

1295ᵇ13. Besides all this, those who are enjoying an excess of the gifts of fortune, strength and wealth and friends and the like, neither wish nor know how to be ruled. They become like this while still children at home; for because of their luxury they are not accustomed to be ruled even at school. Those, on the other hand, who are excessively deprived of these things become too humble. Consequently the latter do not know how to rule, but only how to be slavishly ruled, while the former do not know how to be ruled in any way, but only how to rule despotically. Thus arises a city not of free men but of slaves and masters, the one side envious and the other contemptuous. That is at the farthest remove from friendship and political community. For community involves friendliness; men do not wish even to take a journey in common with enemies. The city aims at consisting as much as possible of equal and similar persons, and this state of affairs exists most in the middle class. The best constituted city, therefore, must be the one consisting of those whom we hold to make up the natural composition of a city.

1295ᵇ28. Furthermore, these persons are the most secure citizens in cities. That is because they do not desire other people's property as the poor do, nor do others desire theirs as the poor desire that of the rich. And because they neither plot nor are plotted against they live safely. Phocylides therefore did well to pray: 'I wish to be a middle citizen; many things are best for them.'

1295ᵇ34. It is plain, then, that the best political community also is the one that is through the middle citizens, and that those cities can be well constituted which have a large middle class, preferably stronger than both the other classes together, but at any rate stronger than either of them by itself. This is because by attaching itself to either side it turns the scale and prevents the contrary excesses. It is therefore a very great blessing if the property of the politically active is intermediate and adequate. Where some own a great deal and the rest own nothing, there arises either an ultimate democracy or an unmixed oligarchy, or else a tyranny, which can come from either excess. Tyranny arises both out of the most exuberant democracy and out of oligarchy. It arises far less out of the middle citizens and those close to them. Why this is so I shall say later, in discussing changes of constitution.

1296ᵃ7. It is plain that the middle constitution is the best, for it is the only stable one. Parties and factions occur least among the citizens, when there are many people in the middle. Large cities are more stable for the same reason, namely that the middle class is numerous in them. In small cities it is easy to separate everybody into two, leaving no middle class, and practically everybody is either needy or prosperous.

1296ª13. It is the middle citizens, again, who make democracies safer than oligarchies and more lasting, because they are more numerous in democracies than in oligarchies and have a larger share in the honours. The needy, when their numbers are excessive and there is no middle class, manage things badly and are soon ruined.

1296ª18. The fact that the best legislators have come from the middle class should be regarded as good evidence of this. Solon was one of them, as is clear from his poetry. So were Lycurgus (he was not a king) and Charondas and most of the others.

1296ª22. This explains why most constitutions are either democratic or oligarchic. The middle class in them being frequently small, whoever preponderate at a given time, whether the property-owners or the demos, depart from the middle and draw the constitution towards themselves, so that it becomes either a demos or an oligarchy. Furthermore, the factions and battles that occur between the demos and the prosperous cause whichever of the opponents may happen to get the better not to establish a common or equal constitution, but to take as their reward for victory the control of the constitution, and make either a democracy or an oligarchy. Also, those who have had the leadership in Greece have looked to their home constitutions and established either democracies or oligarchies in the cities, aiming not at the good of the cities but at their own.

1296ª36. Owing to these causes the middle constitution either never or rarely occurs, and in few places. Only one man among former leaders has ever been persuaded to institute this arrangement. And now the inhabitants of the cities are accustomed not even to want equality, but either to aim at ruling or to endure being mastered.

1296ᵇ2. This makes it clear which is the best constitution, and why it is so. As to the other constitutions (since we hold that there are several democracies and several oligarchies), which is to be placed first and second and so on in order of merit is not hard to see now that the best is determined. The nearest to this must always be better, and the one farther away from the middle must be worse, unless one is judging in reference to an hypothesis. I say 'in reference to an hypothesis' because it can often happen that a less desirable constitution is more advantageous for some people.

COMMENT. Aristotle now passes to another of the questions which he proposed in IV 1. He has been dealing in IV 3–10 with the question which I numbered 5 in IV 1, namely how many sorts of constitution there are. He now turns to the question which I numbered 4, namely which constitution most suits all cities. He rephrases it as: which constitution best suits *most* cities? He again emphasizes its practical character; it is an attempt to be useful to ordinary cities.

His answer in this chapter is: 'the middle constitution'. This is a new phrase; and we need to ask ourselves what it means, and what is the relation of the middle constitution to the constitution which we read about in IV 8 and 9, namely the mixed constitution, or 'constitution' in the specific sense.

It is clear that 'the middle constitution' (1296ª37) is the same as 'the political community that is through the middle citizens' (1295ᵇ35). But what is being 'through the middle citizens'? Is it a constitution in which only the middle citizens share, neither the poor *nor the rich* being allowed to attend Assembly or Court? Aristotle's unfavourable comments on the rich in this chapter, ending with the statement that they only know how to rule despotically (1295ᵇ21), make us think for

a moment that he is proposing to deprive them of all political partici-
pation in constitutional as opposed to despotic cities. Yet we conclude
that this is such an extraordinary proposal that, if he had intended it,
he would have said so far more unmistakably. It is much more probable that there is no upper limit to the property that may be owned
by the participator in 'the middle constitution', but a fairly high
lower limit, higher than that in Aristotle's best kind of democracy.

The presence of such a law will not, however, be sufficient to produce Aristotle's 'middle constitution'. As usual, he here means by a
constitution something different from a set of laws, namely a set of
people organized and living in accord with certain laws and customs
and aims; and it is essential to his 'middle constitution' that in fact
there are in it a large number of persons owning a middle amount of
property. If it contains only very rich and very poor persons it is not
a middle constitution whatever its laws may be.

The chapter is much more like political sociology than like what
we call constitutional studies. It is an enthusiastic affirmation of the
political virtues of the middle class; and it recommends the statesman
to do what he can to make the middle class large in his city.

Did Aristotle think of his 'middle constitution' (IV 11) as identical
with his 'mixed constitution' or 'constitution' in the specific sense
(IV 8 and 9)? He never says that they are identical. The mixed constitution is not named in this chapter, nor in the only other place
where the middle constitution is named (V 1, 1302ᵃ14). The word
'constitution' is only once used specifically in IV 11 (1295ᵃ33), and
not so as to connect it with the middle constitution. This silence is
strange if he means them to be the same. Since he has passed on to a
new question in this chapter, and is no longer giving the answer in the
course of which he wrote of the mixed constitution, he needs to be
explicit on the point if he is to be clearly understood as meaning by
'the middle constitution' what he formerly meant by 'the mixed constitution' or 'constitution'.

In spite of this mysterious silence, interpreters all conclude that the
middle constitution of this chapter is intended to be the same as the
mixed constitution of chapters 8–9, for the following reasons.

(1) Aristotle recommends the 'middle' constitution here, and he
appeared to be recommending the 'mixed' constitution in IV 8–9,
though spoiling his own plan of procedure by doing so. It is unlikely
that he would recommend two different moderate constitutions in the
same book without saying which to prefer.

(2) He says in this chapter that the middle constitution rarely or

never occurs, and 'only one man among former leaders has ever been persuaded to institute' it (1296ᵃ37). Similarly, he wrote in IV 9 as if the mixed constitution were a good to be achieved rather than a phenomenon to be observed.

(3) By the 'middle' constitution he understands here not merely the constitution that is 'through the middle citizens', but also the constitution that is middle between oligarchy and democracy; that is the point of 1296ᵃ22–36. But being middle between oligarchy and democracy is how in IV 9 he understood being a mixture of oligarchy and democracy, that is, a 'constitution'.

(4) Although the phrase 'middle constitution' did not appear in IV 9, the word 'middle' already did so. Aristotle there regarded his first two principles of mixture as producing a middle (1294ᵃ41, ᵇ2, 5). He held that in a middle thing 'each of the extremes is discernible [and] this happens in regard to the Spartan constitution' (1294ᵇ18). And he tended towards the view that a mixture of two things is always a middle between two extremes, and hence that 'constitution' is a middle between two extremes.

(5) Aristotle held that every constitution can be properly called by one of the six names, kingship, aristocracy, 'constitution', democracy, oligarchy, tyranny (cf. 1279ᵇ34). Therefore he held that the middle constitution is one of these six. Which one? It can only be 'constitution'.

In truth 'middle' is a better name for what Aristotle proposes than is 'mixture'. He proposes that eligibility for office be given to a middle amount of citizens, more than it is given to in oligarchy but less than it is given to in democracy. This is truly a middle in an obvious literal sense. But it is a mixture only metaphorically, or by the false principle that every middle is a mixture.

Who were Aristotle's middle class? Newman wrote that they 'are, of course, not to be confounded with a modern "middle class" ' (I 500); but he did not tell us either who they were or who the modern middle class is. The modern conception of a middle class is very vague. While it is certain that nearly all lawyers and medical men belong to it, there are great numbers of persons whom we are uncertain whether to put in the middle or in one of the extreme classes, though we know perfectly well which of the extremes they are in if they are in either. Aristotle defines his middle class by reference to property, as being those who are neither very rich nor very poor; but he does not give us much indication where he draws the lines. The definition implies that they include those 'farmers and possessors of moderate property' who control the constitution in the best form of democracy (1292ᵇ25). That is, they include farmers who are at least moderately prosperous. Whether any profession fell almost entirely within Aristotle's middle class I cannot tell. Most professions would probably be partly middle class and partly not. Many men of business would be inside it; but Plato's Cephalus would be too rich to be inside it. The extent to which definite classes exist in a society depends on the extent to which people change or can change their social status.

We learn elsewhere that in a 'constitution' the political community consists of those who carry full arms (II 6, 1265ᵇ28; III 7, 1279ᵇ4), and ought to consist of them alone (IV 13, 1297ᵇ1). (Athenian soldiers provided their own arms, sometimes even their own food.) Some of these remarks sound almost as if Aristotle were defining 'constitution' by reference to a man's arms; but it is his intention to define it by reference to a man's property. We therefore expect him to say that the property-qualification ought to be high enough to ensure that every sharer in the constitution can afford full arms. Instead of that, however, he says it ought to be high enough to make the sharers more numerous than those who do not share (1297ᵇ5).

This chapter has a few remarkable sentences concerning liberty and equality and fraternity (1295ᵇ21–26). He holds each of them to be politically important; and he connects them with the middle constitution, not with democracy as we do. (In his *Ethics*, where he calls 'constitution' by the unambiguous name of 'timocracy', he says that timocracy is like the relation between brothers, 1161ᵃ4.) The city aims at consisting as much as possible of equal and similar persons; but nowadays the inhabitants of the cities are accustomed not even to want equality, but either to aim at ruling or to endure being mastered (1296ᵇ1). This implies that we ought to want equality and aim at it. To cease wondering how Aristotle could sincerely say this when he always excluded from all politics all women and slaves, and here proposes to exclude also the poor, it is enough to remind ourselves that we also exclude some beings from politics. We exclude children, or foreigners, or convicts, or madmen, or peers of the realm, or dogs, or whales. There is always some being just outside the pale, whose inclusion seems imperative to some and absurd to others. There is always a pale. Anyhow, Aristotle is profoundly right that we ought to want equality. Equality is a far better thing than either pagan pride or Christian humility. Or, if you prefer, Christian brotherhood is a far better thing than Christian humility. This is social equality, the habit of treating every sentient being as one whose feelings and wishes are to be respected, and as a fellow sufferer in the miseries of existence, no matter how inferior he may be in intellect or will or capacity to express himself.

Whether Aristotle's middle class really had these political advantages, or would have had them if it had existed, is more than I can tell. Modern middle classes seem to care much more about liberty than they do about equality or fraternity. Fraternity is more characteristic of the poor. Aristotle is certainly right that a sharp division into very rich and very poor is bad for a city, and therefore a middle class is desirable; but this consideration calls for the replacement of definite classes by a long series of degrees, rather than for the addition of a third definite class to two already existing.

Anyhow, his arguments for the middle constitution from the advantages of the middle class are much better than his initial argument (1295^{a}36 ff.) from the definition of happiness in his *Ethics*. That theory was that happiness mainly consists in good action, and good action is not extreme but mean. If this is to be analogically transferred from the man to the city, the conclusion will be that the happy and good city is one that is active in a mean and not an extreme way. It will, for example, conquer the right amount of other cities, neither too many nor too few. What Aristotle draws from the analogy, however, is that the happy and good city will have a large and politically influential middle class. This does not follow because it is nothing to do with action.

IV 12. SUMMARY. *What constitution suits a given people depends on the proportion there between the superiority of one part to another in quality and its inferiority to that other in quantity. The legislator should always include the middle class in the political community.*

TRANSLATION. 1296^{b}13. The next question is what constitution suits what people and what sort of constitution suits what sort of people. We must first lay down one general principle covering all of them: the part of the city that wishes the constitution to remain as it is ought to be stronger than the part that does not so wish.

1296^{b}17. Now every city is made up of quality and quantity. By 'quality' I mean freedom, wealth, education, and birth; by 'quantity' I mean superiority in number. It can happen that, while the quality belongs to one of the parts of which the city consists and the quantity belongs to another (for example, the ignoble more numerous than the noble, or the needy more numerous than the rich), the excess in quantity is not so great as the defect in quality. In that case they must be judged against each other. Where the number of the needy exceeds the stated proportion, there democracy is natural, and the particular kind of democracy that accords with the excess of that particular demos. For example, if the farmers exceed in numbers it will be the first democracy, if the workmen and wage-earners the last. And similarly with the others that lie between these. But where the class of the prosperous and notable exceeds in quality more than it falls behind in quantity, there oligarchy is natural, and, as before, the particular kind of oligarchy that accords with the superiority of that oligarchic class.

1296^{b}34. The legislator should always include the middle citizens in the political community. If he is making the laws oligarchic, he should aim at the middle citizens; and, if democratic, he should gain them with his laws.

1296^{b}38. Where the middle class exceeds the two extremes together, or even only one of them, there a constitution can be enduring. For there is no fear of the rich ever concerting with the poor against them, because neither of these parties will ever want to serve the other, and if they look for a constitution more in their common interest than this they will not find it. They would not consent to rule by turns because they distrust each other. Everywhere the arbiter is the person most trusted; and the man in the middle is an arbiter.

1297^{a}6. The better the constitution is mixed, the more

durable it is. Many even of those who want to construct aristocratic constitutions make the mistake not merely of giving more to the prosperous, but also of misleading the demos. False goods inevitably give rise sooner or later to a true evil. And the encroachments of the rich do more to destroy the constitution than those of the demos.

COMMENT. Aristotle passes on again, this time to the question which I numbered 2 in chapter 1, now expressed as 'what constitution suits what people and what sort of constitution suits what sort of people'.

There are several puzzles here: (1) What exactly is the 'proportion', and where did we 'state' it (1296ᵇ25)? Perhaps Aristotle is assuming that it is possible to grade degrees of culture numerically, and imagining an equation or inequation of the following form,

$$\frac{\text{number of poor}}{\text{number of rich}} \gtrless \frac{\text{culture of rich}}{\text{culture of poor}},$$

and meaning to say that democracy is natural where the lefthand ratio is the greater, and oligarchy is natural where the righthand ratio is the greater. Perhaps the 'stated proportion', though it has not really been stated, is the case where the two ratios are equal, which is the only case in which the four terms make a proportion.

(2) The answer is in terms of what is 'natural'; the question was in terms of what 'suits', and of what 'fits' in its original statement in IV 1. All three terms seem to involve that Aristotle is making a recommendation. The question therefore arises how this recommendation is related to the recommendation of the middle constitution in IV 9 and 11; and that is the second puzzle raised by this chapter. How can he both recommend the middle constitution for most cities, and recommend democracy for some and oligarchy for others? The present chapter seems to leave to the middle constitution only the case where the two ratios are equal. This case will probably occur far less frequently than the cases where the ratios are unequal. Hence the middle constitution will not be best for most cities but only for a small minority of them.

The only solution I can think of is to suppose that Aristotle is not speaking of every deviation from the proportion, but only of very great deviations therefrom. It is only for very great excesses of the number of the poor that he recommends democracy, I will suppose; and only for very great excesses of the culture of the rich that he recommends oligarchy. This will leave him still recommending the middle constitution for most cities, as he does in IV 9 and 11.

(3) It is a doubtful question whether Aristotle in the second half of this chapter means 'constitution' in the generic or the specific sense. Newman I 501 thought he meant it specifically: 'We look for the mention of a definite form of constitution in this passage, for not only are democracy and oligarchy mentioned in the corresponding sentences, 1296^{b}26, 32, but the question under consideration is' what constitution suits what people. This is a strong reason. And another is that the word 'this' in 1297^{a}3 looks much like a reference to the specific 'constitution'.

There are, however, strong reasons on the other side also. Against Newman's contrast with the first half of the chapter we must note that oligarchy and democracy are still being mentioned in the second half of the chapter (1296^{b}36–37). Against his thought that we look for the mention of a definite form of constitution here (that is, one of the six), we must note that the constitution Aristotle recommended in the previous chapter was not referred to as any of the six, but as 'the middle constitution'. And I give great weight to the principle that Aristotle's word 'constitution' means constitution in general whenever it can, and means the specific 'constitution' only when it must do so, either because it is preceded by the words 'the so called' or because of something else in the context.

I admit, of course, that there do exist generically-specifically ambiguous words which mean the species unless compelled by the context to mean the genus. 'Corruption' is one of these in modern political English; it means the species venality unless compelled by its context to mean corruption in general. Another is 'cat'; it means the domestic species unless compelled to mean the genus, as in the sentence 'a lynx is a cat'. But I believe that other generically-specifically ambiguous words exist which mean the genus unless compelled by the context to mean the species, and that Aristotle's word 'constitution' is one of these.

I interpret 'constitution' in this chapter, though not without fear that I may be wrong, as always meaning the genus.

The first half of the chapter works with a division of the city into two classes, the rich and the poor. The second half returns to the threefold division of the previous chapter, and again presses the middle class upon the legislator. It does not, however, return to the middle constitution, or at least does not unmistakably do so. It mentions oligarchy and democracy, and recommends getting the middle class to participate in each of these. It does not use the word 'constitution' in the specific sense. It does not name the 'middle' constitution. And its single reference to the constitution's being better 'mixed' (1297ᵃ6) is not confined to the cases where the constitution is specifically a 'constitution'.

IV 13. SUMMARY. *Rules regarding attendance at Assembly and Court should make rich and poor both come. The political community should consist only of those having heavy arms.*

TRANSLATION. 1297ᵃ14. The pretences which they invent against the demos in the constitutions are five in number. They have to do with Assembly, with the offices, with courts, with armour, with training. (1) As regards Assembly, the right of Assembly to belong to all, but the prosperous to be penalized for not attending, and either only the prosperous or a much greater penalty for them. (2) As regards the offices, those with rateable property not allowed to swear off, but the needy allowed. (3) As regards the courts, the prosperous penalized for not attending, but the needy scotfree; or else the former a big penalty and the latter a small one, as in the laws of Charondas. Sometimes all who have registered may attend Assembly and the courts, but if having registered they fail to attend either Assembly or the courts they incur big penalties, in order that the penalty may prevent them from registering, and not registering may prevent them from attending. They make similar laws about owning arms and taking training: (4) the needy are permitted not to own them, but the prosperous are liable to a penalty if they do not own them; (5) similarly, if they do not train, the former suffer no penalty but the prosperous are liable to one. This is in order that the one class may take part because of the penalty, and the others may not take part because they have nothing to fear. These are oligarchic devices in legislation.

1297^{a}35. In the democracies they have counterdevices. They provide pay for the needy who attend Assembly and Court, and they impose no fine on the prosperous. Plainly, therefore, if one wants to mix fairly, one should bring together the devices of each party, providing pay for the one and penalty for the other. This would make everyone join in, whereas the other way makes the political community consist of one side only.

1297^{b}1. The political community should consist of those having heavy arms only. On the other hand, it is not possible to define absolutely the amount of the assessment that a man should have. Instead we must examine what is the largest amount that will still make those who share in the community outnumber those who do not, and fix it at that. The poor will keep quiet even without sharing in the honours, provided no one outrages them or takes away any of their property. (This, however, is not easy; for those who have a part in the government do not always happen to be courteous.) And when there is a war they usually hang back, if they do not receive food and are in need; if someone provides food, they will fight.

1297^{b}12. In some places the political community consists not only of those who carry heavy arms but also of those who have done so. This was so among the Maleans, but they chose the officers from the active soldiers. The first political community that arose in Greece after the kingships consisted of the fighting men. These were originally the knights, because the strength and superiority in war lay with the knights. Heavily armed infantry are useless without formation, but the ancients had no experience of ranks and such matters; that is why their strength lay in the knights. But as cities grew and the men at arms got more power the political community grew larger. That is why what we now call 'constitutions' were formerly called democracies. The ancient communities were, of course, oligarchic and kingly. Being small they had little middle class, and it submitted to being ruled because it was small in numbers and bad at organization.

1297ᵇ28. We have now said for what reason there are several constitutions, and why there are others besides the recognized ones (democracy is not single in number, nor are the others), also what their differences are and why they arise, and also which of the constitutions is best in the majority of cases, and of the others which suits which men.

COMMENT. In this chapter Aristotle's word 'constitution' is again difficult to interpret. It must mean the specific constitution in the sentence 'what we now call "constitutions" were formerly called democracies' (1297ᵇ24); and there are several places where it certainly means the genus. But which does it mean in 1297ᵇ13, 14, 16, 23, and 25?

I take it to mean the genus. Moreover, I take it to mean the genus in the concrete sense, the political community bound together by a constitution. Hence I translate these five occurrences by 'community' or 'political community'.

My reasons are these. (1) The principle that the word means the genus whenever it can. (2) The passage is concerned to recommend that only the armed citizens share in the constitution. It is not concerned, or at least not primarily concerned, to recommend one of the six constitutions as such.

(3) If the passage were about the specific 'constitution', it would involve a remarkable change of opinion about the frequency of the specific 'constitution'. In IV 9 and 11 the implication was very strong that 'constitution' hardly or never occurs, and is something to be invented in the future rather than inspected in the present or past. But here he would be saying that 'constitution' is found in some places, that the Maleans had it, and that in general it was what succeeded monarchy in the ancient cities of Greece.

This third argument is weakened by the fact that in Book V he does talk as if specific 'constitutions' frequently occurred. But it is more likely that this change of implication comes between the two books than that it comes within Book IV and within his recommendations for ordinary cities.

I conclude that in Aristotle's opinion specific 'constitution' requires that sharing in the generic constitution be confined to the men at arms; but the converse is unnecessary. A constitution confined to the men at arms need not be specifically a 'constitution', and those actual constitutions of men at arms which he refers to (1297^b12–28) were not so.

On the general question whether Aristotle, in using his word 'constitution' to indicate a species of constitution, thinks of himself as referring to an ideal or to a fact, I conclude from Book V that he certainly thought that 'constitutions' had often occurred, but I also conclude from Book IV that he thought of himself as there recommending a particular kind of 'constitution' which had never or rarely occurred.

It is curious that he takes so long to get to the men at arms in answering his practical questions in Book IV. They must have been in his mind throughout, for they were associated with the original definition of specific 'constitution' in III 7, and even earlier in II 6.

Are Aristotle's recommendations in Book IV consistent with those he gave us in Book III? Not entirely. The one best man, at whose appearance we were told in Book III to abandon our constitution and gladly obey, is consistent enough. He is not mentioned in Book IV; but we may well suppose that he remains in the back of Aristotle's mind, a genuine exception to what he here says, but so rare as not to require mention again. The rule of law, which Book III recommended for all ordinary situations, is no doubt still recommended here, though tacitly. There does, however, appear to be a change of view on the proper extent of eligibility to office, which he calls sharing in the constitution. It is now to be confined to those who can afford arms. Book III, on the contrary, said that 'a city in which there are many poor men excluded from office must be full of enemies' (1281^b30), and recommended giving the poor the right to serve in the Assembly and the Courts. Book III seems a little more favourable to the masses than Book IV. However, the proposition mainly intended in Book III was perhaps that democracy is better than oligarchy; and this is consistent with the proposition suggested by Book IV, that 'constitution' in the specific sense is better than democracy.

The conception of 'political goodness' was prominent in Book III but does not appear in Book IV. In Book III Aristotle said that political goodness gave the best right to rule. In Book IV he wants the middle class to rule; but he does not say they have political goodness; he only says the best legislators have come from them. The good consequences which he expects from their predominance are consequences which they do not personally intend, and not the aims of their wisdom.

IV 14-16. MODES OF APPOINTING OFFICERS

IV 14. SUMMARY. *Every constitution has three parts, that which deliberates about public affairs, that which concerns the offices, and the judging part. There are various modes of appointing the deliberative part. Different modes belong to different constitutions. Recommendations.*

TRANSLATION. 1297^{b}35. Now let us discuss what comes next, both generally and with respect to each constitution separately. The appropriate starting point is this: every constitution has three parts with regard to which the good legislator must consider its advantage; if they are in a good state the constitution must be in a good state; and constitutions differ from each other in the differences of each of these parts. Of these three one is: (1) What is the part that deliberates about public affairs? A second is (2) that which concerns the offices, that is to say, what they should be and what they should control, and how they should be filled. A third is: (3) What is the judging part?

1298^{a}3. (1) The deliberative part controls war and peace, alliance and disalliance, laws, death and exile and confiscation, and the choice of officers and their audits. Either (1. 1) all these decisions must be given to all the citizens, or (1. 2) all to some of them (for example, to some one office or to several, or some to some and others to others), or (1. 3) some of them to all and others to some.

1298^{a}9. (1. 1) For all the citizens to decide, and about all matters, is democratic; that kind of equality is what the demos wants. It can be done in several ways. (1. 11) One way is for them to take turns, and not to act all together in a body. This is so in the constitution of Telecles the Milesian; and there are other constitutions in which the deliberative body is the officers jointly, but everyone holds office in turn from all the tribes and the least parts, until it has gone through everyone. In this mode there is a full Assembly only for legislation and constitutional matters, and to hear the announcements of the officers.

1298ª19. (1. 12) Another way is for them to act all together in a body, but to meet only for elections, legislation, war and peace, and audits, other matters being deliberated on by the officers appointed to deal with them, these officers being taken from all, either by election or by lot.

1298ª24. (1. 13) Another way is for the citizens to meet to discuss the elections and the audits, also war and alliance, other matters being managed by the officers, and the officers being elected if possible, that is, such as require knowledge.

1298ª28. (1. 14) A fourth way is for all to meet and deliberate about all matters, and for the officers to decide nothing but merely prepare it. This is what happens now in the ultimate democracy, which we say is analogous to dynastic oligarchy and to tyrannical monarchy. All these ways are democratic.

1298ª34. (1. 2) For some of the citizens to make all of the decisions is oligarchic. This too has several modes. (1. 21) When they are eligible on moderate assessments, and are numerous because of the moderation of the assessment, and they follow the law and do not make changes where it forbids them to do so, and everyone who has the assessment may take part, that is an oligarchy, but it is a 'constitutional' one in virtue of its moderation. (1. 22) When not everybody takes part in deliberation but only elected persons, and they rule in accordance with law as previously, that is oligarchic. (1. 23) When those in control of deliberation choose themselves, and son succeeds to father and they control the laws, this is necessarily a most oligarchical arrangement.

1298ᵇ5. (1. 3) When some of the decisions are given to some of the citizens, for example, when all decide about war and peace and audits but other matters are decided by officers, and these officers are made by election not by lot, the constitution is an aristocracy. If elected officers decide some matters and allotted officers decide others, and the latter are allotted either simply or out of preselected persons, or if elected and allotted officers decide jointly, this partakes partly of an aristocratic constitution and partly of 'constitution' itself.

1298ᵇ11. Those are the divisions of the deliberative part that concern constitutions; and each constitution conducts it in the way indicated.

1298ᵇ13. In the kind of democracy that is considered to be most truly a democracy nowadays (I mean the one in which the demos is supreme even over the laws), it contributes to better deliberation if they do the same as is done with regard to the courts in oligarchies. Oligarchs prescribe a penalty for those whom they wish to act as judges to make them do so; and democrats give pay to the needy. It is useful to do this regarding the assemblies also; for they will deliberate better if they all do it together, the demos along with the notables, and the latter along with the mass. It is also useful if the deliberators are elected, or allotted in equal numbers from the parts. And it is useful, especially if the democratic citizens exceed greatly in numbers, either not to give pay to all, but to as many as is commensurate with the number of the notables, or to exclude the excess by lot.

1298ᵇ26. In oligarchies it is useful either to coopt some persons from the mass, or to establish a board like the so called Precouncillors and Lawguards who exist in some constitutions, and then deal only with matters predeliberated by these officers. Thus the demos will share in deliberation, but will not be able to undo anything that concerns the constitution. Also that the demos either votes what has been put before it, or nothing contrary thereto; or else to let all advise, but only the officers deliberate.

1298ᵇ34. The opposite of what actually happens in the constitutions is what ought to be done. The majority ought to be made supreme in rejecting a measure, but not supreme in adopting it; in the latter case let it be referred back to the officers. But they do the converse in the constitutions: the few are supreme in rejecting and not supreme in adopting; when they adopt anything it is always referred to the majority. So much for the deliberative and sovereign part of the constitution.

COMMENT. 'Every constitution has three parts with regard to which the good legislator must consider its advantage.' We have previously had parts of the city, but not parts of the constitution. Aristotle does not say whether a constitution must have only these three parts, or may have more, or must have more. But in the next chapter he decides that many of the 'functionaries' of the constitution are not 'officers' of the constitution, which probably implies that the constitution has more parts than these three, but the rest are less important.

What are parts of a constitution? They are not classes or groups or professions in a society; those are parts of a city, not of a constitution. They are not paragraphs in a piece of writing. They are probably officers or colleges of officers recognized and maintained by the constitution as part of the government of the city. More simply, they are parts of the government. They are not necessarily embodied in distinct persons; for example, in the Athenian democracy the deliberators and the judges are the same persons.

Aristotle's trichotomy is by no means clear. He introduces his first and third parts by referring to their specific functions: the first is 'the part that deliberates about public affairs' and the third is 'the judging part'. But deliberation is not specific to any officer or college of officers; they all do it. And Aristotle later explicitly recognizes that his second part does it (1299ᵃ26). Furthermore, he here at once assigns to his 'deliberative part' many functions which are not deliberation but decision (1298ᵃ4–7). Evidently he has not achieved an accurate description, at least of his first part.

What Aristotle really means by 'the deliberative part' seems to be the biggest official body in the city, for instance the Assembly at Athens. This chapter is largely a consideration of various ways in which authority may be divided between the Assembly and the officers. These various ways are considered with respect to their suitability to each of the four constitutions, democracy, oligarchy, aristocracy, and 'constitution'. Kingship and tyranny are not mentioned, and aristocracy is hardly distinguished from 'constitution'.

'The deliberative part controls war and peace, alliance and dis-alliance, laws, death and exile and confiscation, and the choice of officers and their audits.' This sentence seems to contradict a great deal of the rest of the chapter. For instance, it contradicts: 'Another way is for them . . . to meet only for elections, legislation, war and peace, and audits, other matters being deliberated on by the officers appointed to deal with them.' In that way the deliberative part does *not* control alliance and disalliance, or death and exile and confiscation, contrary to this sentence. We must suppose that 'controls' is a loose way of saying 'sometimes controls'.

Aristotle's triad is not the same as Locke's or Montesquieu's; and neither of these men appeals to Aristotle for his triad, although Montesquieu frequently appeals to the *Politics* on other points. Locke's three parts are the legislative, the executive, and the federative (which conducts foreign relations). Here only his executive is one of Aristotle's parts; for Aristotle's deliberative is not wholly or even essentially legislative, nor is it wholly or even essentially concerned with foreign relations (*Second Treatise of Civil Government*, cc. xi, xii). Montesquieu's three parts are the legislative, the executive (which appears to confine itself to foreign policy), and the judiciary (*Esprit des Lois* XI vi: De la Constitution d'Angleterre). Here only the judiciary is one of Aristotle's parts. Montesquieu's chief reason for introducing his triad is to insist that liberty requires that no two of these three 'powers' be invested in the same persons, a point which Aristotle does not make. Montesquieu and Locke are talking about functions or powers; but Aristotle is talking mainly about official bodies.

Any number of other political triads can of course be produced. One of the more interesting is T. A. Sinclair's: 'There are in fact three groups—the government, those employed by the government, and the rest of the population. Since these are the necessary components of any State, the difference between one and another will depend largely on the composition of each group and the powers which it can exercise in relation to the others' (*A History of Greek Political Thought*, p. 151).

It is just possible that Aristotle intended IV 14–16 as an answer to the sixth question of IV 1, which was which laws are the best and which laws fit each of the constitutions. There is no other question listed in IV 1 or IV 2 to which IV 14–16 is a conceivable answer.

IV 15. SUMMARY. *It is difficult to say precisely which functionaries are officers. Offices may be combined in small cities which have to be separated in large cities. Some offices are peculiar to certain constitutions. The modes of appointing officers, and their constitutional affinities.*

TRANSLATION. 1299ᵃ3. (2) Next comes the division of offices. This part of the constitution also admits many differences: how many offices there are, what their powers are, and with regard to time, how long each office is held (some make the offices halfyearly, some less, some yearly, some longer); and whether the offices should be perpetual, or of long duration, or neither of these but the same people should hold them several times, or not twice but once only; further about the appointment of the officers, who are to be eligible and who are to choose them and how. With regard to each of these one should be able, first, to distinguish how many modes it admits, and then to assign each sort to the sort of constitution it suits.

1299ᵃ14. Even to decide which are to be called offices is by no means easy. The political community requires many functionaries, so that we cannot regard as an officer everyone who is appointed by vote or by lot. For example,

the priests, in the first place—priesthood has to be regarded as something other than a political office. Patrons
of the drama, too, and heralds, are elected, and so are
ambassadors. Functions are either political (and these
either concern all the citizens with regard to one enterprise,
as being commander in a war, or concern a part of them,
as being superintendent of women or of children), or
economic (for they often elect grain-rationers), or menial
(and to these, if they are prosperous, they appoint slaves).
Generally speaking, officers most properly so called are
those who are responsible for deliberating about certain
matters, deciding them, and giving orders, and especially
the last. To give orders is particularly characteristic of an
officer. This question has scarcely any practical importance
(since no one has yet gone to law about the word); but
there is some intellectual work to be done on it.

1299ᵃ31. More important are the questions which
offices, and how many of them, are necessary to the existence of a city, and which offices, while not necessary, are
useful for a good constitution. These questions are important for every constitution, but particularly so for
small cities. In large cities it is both possible and right
to have one office for one function; many people can take
office because there are many citizens, and each will hold
a given office either once only or after a long interval, and
every function is better done when the person in charge
has no other business. In small cities, however, many
offices have to be collected into few officers. The lack of
men makes it hard for many to be in office; for who will
be their successors? Yet sometimes the small cities need
the same offices and laws as do the big. Whereas, however,
the big cities need them often, the small cities need them
only at long intervals. Hence there is nothing to prevent

their imposing many duties together, since they will not interfere with each other, and the lack of men compels them to make their offices like spitlamps.[1] If therefore we can say how many offices every city must have, and how many it need not but ought to have, one knowing these things would more easily collect which offices it is fitting to collect into one office.

1299^{b}14. It is also fitting not to forget this, namely, which matters should be taken care of by many local offices, and which should be under one supreme control everywhere. Thus, does good behaviour require a controller of the market in the market and another officer elsewhere, or the same one everywhere? And should we divide with regard to the work or with regard to the persons; I mean, for example, one for good behaviour, or another one for children and women? Also, with regard to the constitutions, does the nature of the offices differ in each of them, or not at all? In democracy and oligarchy and aristocracy and monarchy, are the same offices supreme, though not filled from equal or like persons, but from different persons in different constitutions (from the educated in aristocracies, from the rich in oligarchies, and from the free in democracies); or are certain of the offices determined precisely by the differences in the constitutions, sometimes the same and sometimes different ones being advantageous? (Since it is fitting for the same office to be large in some places and small in others.)

1299^{b}30. Some offices are indeed peculiar to particular constitutions. Such is that of the Precouncillors; for it is not democratic. A Council is democratic, since there needs to be something of the kind whose duty it will be to

---

[1] Apparently a military tool that could be used either as a cooking-spit or as a lampstand.

predeliberate for the demos, in order that it may attend to its affairs. But, if this body is small in numbers, it is oligarchic; and Precouncillors are necessarily few in quantity and hence oligarchic. Where both these offices exist, the Precouncillors stand over the Councillors; for the Councillor is democratic and the Precouncillor oligarchic. The power of the Council is also dissolved in those democracies where the demos itself meets and does all the business. This usually happens when there is plenty of money to pay people for attending. They then have the leisure to meet frequently and decide everything for themselves.

1300ª4. The superintendent of children, and the superintendent of women, and any other officer there may be charged with a similar duty, are aristocratic. They are not democratic; for how can one prevent the women of the poor from going out? Nor are they oligarchic; for the women of oligarchs are luxurious. So much for these matters at present.

1300ª9. Let us try to go through the appointment of officers from the beginning. The differences lie in three marks, which when put together must include all the modes. These three are, first (2. 1), who appoint the officers, second (2. 2), from whom do they appoint them, and, lastly (2. 3), how? Each of these three subdivides into three. Either (2. 11) all the citizens appoint or (2. 12) some of them. And they do so either (2. 21) from all the citizens or (2. 22) from those determined in some way, as by assessment or family or goodness or the like. Thus at Megara it is those who returned and fought the demos in a body. And the appointment may be either (2. 31) by election or (2. 32) by lot. And again combined, I mean that (2. 13) the appointers may be some of the citizens for some officers but all of them for others, and (2. 23) those eligible may be all of the citizens for some offices but some of them for others, and (2. 33) some of the officers may be appointed by election and others by lot.

1300ª22. There will be six modes of each difference of these. Either all appoint from all by election; or all appoint from all by lot; or all appoint from some by election; or all appoint from some by lot (and, if from all, either by turns, for instance according to tribes and demes and brotherhoods, until it has gone through all the citizens, or from all every time); or sometimes one way and sometimes the other. Again, if the appointers are some of the citizens, they may appoint either from all by election, or from all by lot, or from some by election, or from some by lot, or sometimes one way and sometimes the other. I mean sometimes from all by election, sometimes by lot, and sometimes from some by election, sometimes by lot. Thus arise twelve modes, besides the two combinations.

1300ª31. Three of these modes of appointment are democratic, namely when all appoint from all by election, or by lot, or both, that is, some of the offices by lot and some by election. When not all the citizens together appoint, either from all or from some either by lot or by election or both, or some of the offices from all and others from some, either by lot or by election or both (where by 'both' I mean some by lot and others by election), that is 'constitutional'. And where some appoint from all either by election or by lot or by both (some of the offices by lot and some by election) it is oligarchic, 'by both' being more oligarchic.[1] Some of the offices from all and some from some is aristocratically 'constitutional', or some by election and some by lot. Some of the offices from some by election

[1] Reading ἢ ἀμφοῖν, τὰς μὲν κλήρῳ τὰς δ' αἱρέσει, ὀλιγαρχικόν in 1300ª39–40.

is oligarchic. So is some from some by lot (equally so, if it does not occur). So is some from some by both ways. Some from all and all from some by election are aristocratic.

1300ᵇ5. Such is the number of the modes of appointing to office, and the way in which they divide among the constitutions. Which benefit which, and how the appointments should be made, will become clear at the same time as the powers of the offices and what they are. By a power of an office I mean a thing like the control of the revenues and the control of defence. For a power like that of the commander in chief is different in kind from the control of commercial intercourse.

COMMENT. We find here that Aristotle knows that there is obscurity in the description of his second part, 'that which concerns the officers'. He refrains from writing 'the officers', because that expression had a technical sense at Athens which was much narrower than he wants. He means to include far more 'officers' than those technically so called at Athens. On the other hand, he means to exclude the assemblymen, who form his first part, and the judges, who form his third part. He now tells us that he also means to exclude the priests, the patrons of the drama, the heralds, and the ambassadors. Who is left? 'Those who are responsible for deliberating about certain matters, deciding them, and giving orders, and especially the last. To give orders is particularly characteristic of an officer.' Still he probably has not said all that he is thinking. The policeman and the gaoler give orders; but Aristotle would probably exclude them. He is probably thinking of those higher officers who initiate orders, and who are not themselves acting under orders, except metaphorically under the orders of the laws and the Assembly. He is thinking of what the English call 'administrative' rather than 'executive' officers.

IV 16. SUMMARY. *Eight kinds of lawcourt. Modes of appointing judges.*

TRANSLATION. 1300ᵇ13. (3) Last of the three come the judges. We must take the modes of them too on the same principle. There is a difference among courts in three marks: from whom, about what, and how? I mean by from whom, are they taken from all or from some? By about what, how many kinds of court are there? And by how, are they appointed by lot or by election?

1300ᵇ18. First let us distinguish how many kinds of court there are. They are eight in number. One is the court that audits officers. Another is when someone offends against some public interest. Another deals with whatever affects the constitution. A fourth, both for officers and for private persons, deals with disputes about penalties. A fifth deals with private transactions where they are substantial. Besides these there are the homicide court and the strangers' court. The kinds of homicide court, whether having the same judges or not, are for premeditated homicide, for involuntary homicide, for homicide admitted but claimed to be justifiable, and, fourth, for charges against persons exiled for homicide upon their return, such as at Athens the court in Phreatto is said to hear. But such cases are few in the whole of time, even in the big cities. The strangers' court has a part for strangers against strangers, and another for strangers against townsmen. Besides all these there is a court for small transactions involving a drachma or five drachmas or little more. There has to be a decision about these matters too; but it does not fall to a quantity of judges. But let us leave them, and also the homicide and the strangers' courts, and talk of the political courts. If these do not work well divisions arise and changes of the constitutions.

1300ᵇ38. Either they must all judge about all the matters distinguished and be appointed by election, or by lot, or all judge about all the matters and be appointed for some of them by lot and for others by election, or about some matters, the same ones, be appointed some of them by lot and some of them by election. That is four modes; and the sectional modes are as many again. Either the judges are taken from a certain class by election and judge about everything, or they are taken from a certain class by lot and judge about everything, or by lot for some things and by election for others, or some courts are made up of both allotted and elected persons for the same cases. These modes, in the order given, are the counterparts of those previously mentioned. Further, the same combined, I mean the judges appointed from all for some matters and from some for others and from both for others (for example, if the same court were made up partly of judges taken from all and partly of judges taken from some); and either by lot or by election or by both. Such are the possible modes of the courts.

1301ª11. Of these the first are democratic, those where they are taken from all and judge about all. The second are oligarchic, those where they are taken from some and judge about all. The third are aristocratic and 'constitutional', those where they are taken from all for some matters and from some for others.

SUPPLEMENTARY ESSAY

DAVID KEYT

1. *Robinson's Interpretation of the* Politics

When this book containing Richard Robinson's limpid translation of, and thoughtful observations on, Books III and IV was originally published in 1962 as the first volume in the Clarendon Aristotle Series, Aristotle's *Politics* had been largely ignored in the English-speaking world for over half a century. This was due partly to a general neglect of political philosophy among British and American philosophers and partly to the long shadow cast by W. L. Newman's monumental four-volume edition and commentary, published in the waning years of Victoria's reign, which seemed to say everything worth saying on the *Politics*.[1] What little study there was of the *Politics* in the middle decades of the twentieth century fell under the influence of the developmental approach to Aristotle initiated by Werner Jaeger[2] and came to focus more on the evolution of Aristotle's political ideas than on the ideas themselves.[3] The original publication of Robinson's slender volume marked the beginning of a revival of philosophical interest in the *Politics*, which, as the

In writing this essay I have drawn on my articles 'Aristotle's Theory of Distributive Justice', in David Keyt and Fred D. Miller, Jr. (eds.), *A Companion to Aristotle's Politics* (Oxford, 1991), and 'Aristotle and Anarchism', *Reason Papers*, no. 18 (Fall, 1993), 133–52.

[1] W. L. Newman, *The Politics of Aristotle*, 4 vols. (Oxford, 1887–1902).

[2] *Aristotle: Fundamentals of the History of his Development*, trans. Richard Robinson, 2nd edn. (Oxford, 1948). The original German edition was published in 1923.

[3] For a brief introduction to Books III and IV written from a developmental perspective see Eckart Schütrumpf, *Aristoteles Politik*, ii (Berlin, 1991), 109–18.

accompanying bibliography makes plain, is now in full flood. The accuracy and lucidity of Robinson's translation made the central books of the *Politics* more accessible, while his interpretation and forthright criticism shifted the focus back to the philosophy itself. One ironic result of the increasing study of the *Politics*, however, has been to cast doubt on many of the things Robinson says about it.

Although Robinson claims that 'the *Politics* is the greatest work there is in political philosophy' (p. xii), he never makes clear what its greatness consists in. He says, for example, that 'the *Politics* is a collection of long essays and brief jottings pretending to be a treatise' (p. ix). He thinks that Aristotle prefers reporting the political principles of others to adopting political principles of his own (p. 70). The positive ideas he finds in Books III and IV are few and mostly commonplace: that '[d]ifferent sorts of peoples require different sorts of constitution' (p. 65); that absolute kingship is sometimes justified (p. 48), though 'for all ordinary situations' the rule of law is best (p. 110); that 'constitution' in the specific sense is better than democracy, which in turn is better than oligarchy (p. 110). Moreover, Robinson is a fierce opponent of Aristotle's naturalism and paternalism, the latter of which he calls 'the most fundamental and most grave error in Aristotle's politics' (p. xxii). Robinson's account of the *Politics* is curiously at odds with his evaluation of it.

It is worth considering whether an alternative interpretation, consonant with the greatness of the *Politics*, is possible. I shall try to show below that in the *Politics* Aristotle is more concerned to develop his own ideas than to report the ideas of others, that Book III contains an elaborate and coherent political philosophy of great subtlety rather than a series of brief jottings on political topics, and that Aristotle's so-called paternalism is sensible social policy.

The systematic nature of Aristotle's political philosophy is difficult to discern because of the way it is presented. Aristotle makes it hard in a number of ways for his reader to see exactly what his political philosophy is and how its parts fit together. It is often difficult to decide whether he is endorsing an idea or merely reporting it, and the order of chapters does not always reflect the logical progression of his thought.[4] But in Book III at least there is a central idea threading its way through his labyrinthine discussion, an idea that he wishes to develop and to which most of the topics in Book III are tied. This idea is distributive justice (see III. 9. 1280ª9–25, 12. 1282ᵇ14–23).[5] Aristotle explains it in a brief chapter of his essay on justice, one of the common books of the *Nicomachean* and *Eudemian Ethics* (*EN* V = *EE* IV), and then uses it as the foundation of an argument in *Politics* III.

2. Distributive Justice

In his chapter on distributive justice, *EN* V. 3, Aristotle pursues the notion, picked up from Plato (see *Gorgias* 507e6–508a8 and *Laws* VI. 756e9–758a2), that distributive justice is a kind of geometric proportion (*EN* V. 3. 1131ᵇ12–13) involving at least two persons, A and B, and two things, C and D (*EN* V. 3. 1131ª18–20). In a just distribution, according to this view, the ratio of C to D is the same as that of A to B:

$$(1) \qquad \frac{A}{B} = \frac{C}{D}.$$

When the ratios are equal, the distribution is just if C is allotted to A, and D to B (*EN* V. 3. 1131ª20–4). To represent this further condition in his formula, Aristotle, calling upon his knowledge of geometry, replaces the ratio of the things by an

---

[4] The division of the various books into chapters does not, of course, go back to Aristotle but is the work of later editors.

[5] All references are to the *Politics* unless otherwise indicated.

equal ratio of sums that reflects 'the yoking together' of A and C and of B and D (*EN* V. 3. 1131^{b}3–12):

(2)
$$\frac{A}{B} = \frac{A + C}{B + D}.$$

A simpler way of accomplishing the same thing would be to replace the dummy names 'C' and 'D' in the original formula by definite descriptions:

(3)
$$\frac{A}{B} = \frac{\text{the thing allotted to } A}{\text{the thing allotted to } B}.$$

But this formula is still unsatisfactory. For, as Aristotle implicitly acknowledges, persons do not stand in ratios to each other *per se* but only in certain respects such as age, height, wealth, and so forth; nor do things. The ratios in Aristotle's formula imply some basis of comparison of the persons and of the things. The basis of comparison of the things is their positive or negative value (*EN* V. 3. 1131^{b}19–23); that of the persons is their worth, or *axia* (*EN* V. 3. 1131^{a}24, 26). Thus, the formula becomes:

(4)
$$\frac{\text{the worth of person } A}{\text{the worth of person } B} = \frac{\text{the value of the thing allotted to } A}{\text{the value of the thing allotted to } B}.$$

The concept of distributive justice, by Aristotle's analysis, asserts that a distribution is just if it follows this formula, if the value of the thing it allots to one person stands to the value of the thing it allots to another as the worth of the one person stands to the worth of the other.[6]

The things distributed by this formula are the apportionable goods: honour, money, and safety (*EN* V. 2. 1130^{b}2, 30–3). The greatest of these in Aristotle's eyes is honour (*EN* IV. 3. 1123^{b}20–1), which includes not only respect and tokens of esteem (*Rhet.* I. 5. 1361^{a}27–^{b}2) but also political office (III.

---

[6] For a detailed analysis of this idea see William A. Galston, *Justice and the Human Good* (Chicago, 1980), 145–50.

10. 1281ª31). Political office is the greatest of the apportionable goods because the political community with its laws regarding political office, property, and military service is the primary arena of distribution, and once the political offices in such a community are distributed these laws and their administration, and hence all further distributions, are under the control of the office-holders.

Disputes about distributive justice break out, Aristotle maintains, not over the principle of distributive justice itself (III. 12. 1282ᵇ18–21, V. 1. 1301ª26–7; *EN* V. 3. 1131ª10–14), nor over the value of the things being distributed (III. 9. 1280ª18–19), but over the worth, or *axia*, of the persons claiming a share of the distribution. 'All agree', Aristotle says, 'that the just in distribution must be according to worth of some sort, though all do not recognize the same sort of worth; but democrats say it is freedom, oligarchs wealth or good birth, and aristocrats virtue' (*EN* V. 3. 1131ª25–8). It is useful here to borrow the distinction from Rawls between the *concept* of distributive justice, which is expressed by the formal and abstract principle of distribution to which everyone assents—formula (4) above—and the various *conceptions* of distributive justice, which evaluate a person's worth according to various standards such as freedom, wealth, good birth, and virtue.[7] Thus, the democratic conception of justice is expressed when worth is evaluated according to the standard of freedom, and the oligarchic conception is expressed when it is evaluated according to the standard of wealth. Everyone shares the same concept of distributive justice, but not the same conception.

Our discussion so far has been based on *EN* V. 3. We must now show how the theory of distributive justice explained in this passage is the key to *Politics* III, beginning with Aristotle's account of citizenship in chapters 1 through 5.

[7] John Rawls, *A Theory of Justice* (Cambridge, Mass., 1971), 5–6, 9–10.

3. Citizenship

Aristotle raises two questions about citizenship. 'We must examine', he says, 'who should be called a citizen and who the citizen is' (III. 1. 1275ª1–2). The first question, which is addressed in III. 1, seeks a functional definition of a citizen proper, a *politēs haplōs* (III. 1. 1275ª5–22). Aristotle's answer is that a citizen proper is a man who is entitled to occupy a certain political office. A citizen proper, he says, is a man who 'is entitled to share in deliberative or judicial office' (III. 1. 1275ᵇ17–19).[8] In a democracy like Athens he is a man who is entitled to sit in the assembly or serve as a juror (III. 1. 1275ª22–33). I shall call such citizens 'full citizens'. The second question, the topic of III. 2, concerns the legal definition of a citizen and asks, not what the job of a citizen is, but who gets the job. Aristotle's answer, reflecting Greek custom, is that a man is a citizen if both his parents were citizens (III. 2. 1275ᵇ22–3).[9]

The second definition implies that not all citizens are proper citizens. For in the Greek world no woman ever held political office; and hence, no woman was ever a citizen proper. But if *both* parents of a citizen proper must be citizens, women must be citizens in some sense. The problem is to explain this sense. Aristotle does not discuss the sense in which a woman can be a citizen, though he does discuss the sense in which a boy can be. He says that a boy or a youth is a citizen 'under an assumption', namely, the assumption that he will one day become a citizen proper (III. 1. 1275ª14–19, 5. 1278ª4–6). The idea seems to be that every sort of citizenship

[8] Retaining, contrary to Ross, the *ē* of all manuscripts.

[9] Aristotle's discussion in chapters 1 and 2 is more ambiguous than my account suggests. In III. 1. 1275ª1–2 he may be posing, not two distinct questions, but one question phrased in two different ways; and in the discussion that follows he may be offering what to his mind is a better and a worse answer to this single question. See Robinson's comment on p. 7.

other than full citizenship is citizenship under an assumption that mentions in some essential way full citizenship. By this idea a female is a citizen, a *politis* as distinct from a *politēs*, 'under the assumption' that she has the legal capacity to transmit (together with a citizen husband) female citizenship to her daughters and full citizenship to her sons.

Another problem emerges in chapter 5 when Aristotle raises the question whether a workman or a labourer who has no share of the political offices in a city should be counted as a citizen. For, as Aristotle says, he is neither a resident alien nor a foreign visitor. So if he is not a citizen, what is he? Aristotle's answer is that he can be a citizen in a democracy (where he can hold office) but not in an aristocracy (where he cannot). But this answer evades the question. What is his status in an aristocracy if he is neither a resident alien nor a foreign visitor? If he has privileges not accorded resident aliens and foreign visitors (such as the right to own land), the answer must be that he is a second-class citizen. In at least two passages Aristotle tacitly recognizes such a concept. In discussing kingship Aristotle, following normal Greek practice, twice refers to some of the king's subjects as citizens (III. 14. 1285^{a}25–9, V. 10. 1311^{a}7–8). (In both passages a citizen, a *politēs*, is contrasted with an alien, a *xenos*.) But no subject of a king holds any deliberative or judicial office unless he is appointed by the king. So by Aristotle's definition of a full citizen there can be only one full citizen in a kingship, the king himself.[10] Anyone else who is a citizen must be a second-class citizen.

On this interpretation of the *Politics* Aristotle divides the population of a typical Greek city into the five following groups (III. 1. 1275^{a}7–8, 2. 1275^{b}37, 5. 1277^{b}38–9; VII. 4. 1326^{a}18–20, ^{b}20–1):

[10] See Newman, i. 230.

  1. First-class citizens:
     a. Full citizens
     b. Immature citizens (III. 1. 1275ª14–19, 5. 1278ª4–6)
     c. Superannuated citizens (III. 1. 1275ª14–19)
     d. Female citizens (III. 2. 1275ᵇ33, 5. 1278ª28)
  2. Second-class citizens
  3. Resident aliens
  4. Foreign visitors
  5. Slaves

Aristotle's discussion of citizenship fleshes out two prelim-
inary matters in the application of his theory of distributive
justice. It contains a definition of the item that, in Aristotle's
view, distributive justice is primarily concerned to distribute,
full citizenship; and it demarcates the group of persons
whose worth, in Aristotle's view and that of the fourth century, should be considered in distributing the item, the free
adult males of a given city.[11]

Having discussed citizenship, Aristotle turns in chapters
6–8 to another topic closely tied to the central idea of distributive justice, that of constitutions.

4. Constitutions

Contrary to some of Robinson's remarks (pp. xv–xvi),
Aristotle's notion of a constitution is virtually identical with
ours. For Aristotle, as for a modern political theorist, a constitution is the structure of the political offices of a political
community, a structure that determines, among other things,
the membership of the community and its end, or goal (III.
1. 1274ᵇ38, 6. 1278ᵇ8–11; IV. 1. 1289ª15–18). Furthermore,
Aristotle distinguishes, just like a modern theorist, between a

[11] By this description of the group, to be free is to be neither an alien nor
a slave. Even though Aristotle never, to my knowledge, explicitly opposes
'free' and 'alien' (*eleutheros* and *xenos*), it is taken for granted in many passages in the *Politics* that the free men under discussion are not aliens.

constitution and the laws made under it (II. 12. 1273ᵇ32–4, 1274ᵇ15–19; III. 11. 1282ᵇ8–13, 15. 1286ᵃ2–4; IV. 1. 1289ᵃ11–25). Robinson is right in noting that for Aristotle a constitution is a way of life (see IV. 11. 1295ᵃ40–ᵇ1), but he is wrong in thinking that this distinguishes Aristotle's conception from ours. Robinson underestimates the extent to which the constitution of a modern state is also a way of life.

'All constitutions', Aristotle says, 'are a kind of justice; for [a constitution] is a community and every community is held together by what is just' (*EE* VII. 9. 1241ᵇ13–15). A constitution is primarily, though not exclusively, a kind of distributive justice. By defining the qualifications for full citizenship, the constitution of a given city is the historical realization of a particular conception of distributive justice. Aristotle's classification of constitutions in chapters 6–8 is thus also a classification of conceptions of distributive justice.

In classifying constitutions Aristotle first divides them into those that are correct and aim at the common advantage, and those that are mistaken and seek only the rulers' own advantage (III. 6. 1279ᵃ17–20, 11. 1282ᵇ8–13). But whose advantage is the common advantage? Aristotle does not give a straightforward answer. The common advantage is not the advantage of every inhabitant of a given city. The common advantage does not include the advantage of slaves (III. 6. 1278ᵇ32–7). Nor apparently does it include the advantage of resident aliens or foreign visitors. Aristotle seems to equate the common advantage in a city with the common advantage of its citizens (III. 13. 1283ᵇ40–2). As Newman remarks, '[t]he common advantage . . . which a State should study is the common advantage of the citizens . . . , and that of other classes, only so far as their advantage is bound up with that of the citizens'.[12] If this is so, we can see the importance of the concept of a

---

[12] Newman, i. 119 n.

second-class citizen for Aristotle's analysis. For first-class citizens all belong to households headed by a full citizen. This means that on the assumption that a man's own advantage is closely tied to that of the household he heads, the advantage of the full citizens of a city will be the same as the advantage of the totality of its first-class citizens. But by Aristotle's definition of a full citizen, the full citizens of a city are its rulers. Hence, if the common advantage of a city were the advantage of its first-class citizens only, a constitution that looks to the common advantage would look only to the rulers' own advantage, and the distinction between correct and deviant constitutions would collapse. The distinction thus implies that a city contains a body of second-class citizens whose advantage is included in the common advantage.[13]

Aristotle initially subdivides correct and deviant constitutions into six kinds by counting the number of rulers: kingship and its perversion, tyranny, have one; aristocracy and its perversion, oligarchy, have only a few; and so-called constitution and its perversion, democracy, have many (III. 7. 1279^{a}25–39, ^{b}4–6). But he quickly abandons this numerical principle in favour of two others, one ethical and one socio-economic (III. 7. 1279^{a}39–^{b}4, 7–10; III. 8). The subdivisions of the two genera now proceed independently, the correct constitutions being subdivided by the ethical principle, virtue, and the deviant constitutions by the socio-economic one, wealth and poverty (or wealth and freedom).[14] These new

[13] A further question about the common advantage is whether it is to be taken as the advantage of the citizens collectively or distributively. For a discussion of this question see John M. Cooper, 'Political Animals and Civic Friendship', in Günther Patzig (ed.), *Aristoteles' 'Politik': Akten des XI. Symposium Aristotelicum* (Göttingen, 1990), 228–41, and Fred D. Miller, Jr. , *Nature, Justice, and Rights in Aristotle's Politics* (Oxford, 1995), 194–204.

[14] Aristotle has difficulty making up his mind whether the mark of democracy is the socio-economic standard, poverty (see III. 7. 1279^{b}8–9, 8. 1279^{b}18–19), or the juristic standard, freedom (see IV. 4. 1290^{b}1, 8. 1294^{a}11; VI. 2. 1318^{a}3–10).

principles are in fact the standards of worth used by the various constitutions in distributing full citizenship. Virtue is the standard of correct constitutions because the rulers under correct constitutions seek the common advantage, and only men of good character will do that. Since virtue comes in various degrees (EN VII. 1. 1144^{a}15–27), there are various kinds of correct constitutions. Heroic virtue is the standard for kingship (I. 12. 1259^{b}10–17, III. 13. 1284^{a}3–12, VII. 14. 1332^{b}16–23); complete virtue for aristocracy; and military (or hoplite) virtue for so-called constitution (III. 7. 1279^{a}37–^{b}4). Wealth and poverty (or wealth and freedom) are the standards for the two perversions, oligarchy and democracy, respectively (III. 8. 1279^{b}34–1280^{a}6; IV. 4. 1290^{b}17–20). Tyranny, which Aristotle is loath to call a constitution at all (IV. 2. 1289^{b}2–3, 8. 1293^{b}27–9), has no standard of worth. (There is no justice of any sort in tyranny.)

It might seem that a broad-based democracy in which every free man is a full citizen should, by Aristotle's analysis, be counted as a correct rather than a mistaken constitution. Under such a constitution the common advantage and the advantage of the full citizens would seem to be identical. In seeking their own advantage, the full citizens would automatically seek the common advantage. Aristotle does not think this will happen. For he believes that a broad-based democracy will always be a proletarian democracy in which the poor outnumber the rich and use their numbers to virtually disenfranchise them (VI. 2. 1317^{b}3–10). By voting against the interests of the rich, the poor in effect turn the juristic standard of democracy, freedom, into the socio-economic standard, poverty, and make the rich second-class citizens.

5. Correct and Mistaken Constitutions

The most important and controversial constitutional idea in Book III and perhaps in the entire treatise is that some constitutions are correct and others mistaken. Thomas Hobbes, for example, thinks such a distinction illusory. '[*Tyranny* and *Oligarchy*]', he says, 'are not the names of other Formes of Government, but of the same Formes misliked. For they that are discontented under *Monarchy*, call it *Tyranny*; and they that are displeased with *Aristocracy*, call it *Oligarchy*.'[15]

There is a good deal more to the distinction between correct and mistaken constitutions than that the rulers under the former seek the common advantage whereas those under the latter seek only their own advantage (III. 6. 1279^{a}17–20). Aristotle claims that correct constitutions are just whereas mistaken ones are not (III. 6. 1279^{a}17–20, 11. 1282^{b}8–13). He thinks that mistaken constitutions are despotic, that the rulers under such constitutions rule their subjects as a master rules slaves rather than as a free man rules other free men (III. 6. 1279^{a}21; see also IV. 3. 1290^{a}25–9 and VII. 14. 1333^{a}3–6). And, as a corollary to the latter idea, he thinks that mistaken constitutions, unlike correct constitutions, are based on force (III. 3. 1276^{a}12–13, 10. 1281^{a}23–4). Aristotle even links the distinction between correct and incorrect constitutions to his naturalism, for he holds that the former are according to nature whereas the latter are contrary to nature (III. 17. 1287^{b}39–41). How do all these ideas fit together? In answering this question we are carried to the very heart of Aristotle's political philosophy.

We can start with the idea that correct constitutions are just whereas mistaken ones are not. Since a constitution is a kind of distributive justice and since the various conceptions of distributive justice differ only in their standards of worth, this idea entails that some standards of worth are correct and others mistaken (see III. 13. 1283^{b}28).

---

[15] *Leviathan* (London, 1651), ch. 19, p. 95.

The search for the correct standard occupies the central chapters of Book III, though the order of the chapters does not follow the steps in Aristotle's argument. The question itself is raised in chapter 10: Who should be supreme in a political community—the many, the rich, the good, the one best man, or a tyrant? Each of the possible answers, Aristotle notes, involves some difficulty, or *aporia*.

Aristotle begins working his way through these difficulties in chapter 12. In a complex argument he rejects the idea that, other things being equal, 'superiority in any good' (height, physical beauty, good complexion, good birth) is a reasonable ground for distributing political offices unequally (1282^b23-7). His first thought is that a rational basis for distributing political office is provided only by those personal qualities that fit a man for political office ($1282^b23-1283^a3$)— namely, justice and political virtue (1283^a20). So the first criterion that Aristotle appeals to in determining the reasonableness of a standard of worth is fitness for the job (1282^b33-4). But later in the chapter he acknowledges the importance of freedom and wealth in a political community and endorses them as reasonable, though not as correct, standards of worth (1283^a14-19). Since Aristotle never argues that free status or wealth fits a man for political office, his idea seems to be that they are reasonable standards of worth because they contribute somehow to a political community. He seems, then, to have introduced a second criterion: contribution to the task (1283^a1; see also III. 9. 1281^a4-8).[16] Aristotle never irons out the relation between his two criteria, and the conflict between them haunts discussions of distributive justice down to our own day. Should ambassadorships, for example, be *rewards* for past service to a political party or *awards* based on diplomatic skills?

---

[16] On these two criteria see Newman, i. 249–50, and Terence Irwin, *Aristotle's First Principles* (Oxford, 1988), 427–8.

A further problem is that the application of both criteria presupposes a conception of the nature of a political community. But the nature of a political community—the sort of enterprise the citizens of a political community are engaged in—is a matter of dispute. Defenders of oligarchy think of a political community as a joint-stock company whose end is to enrich the shareholders (III. 9. 1280^{a}25–31; IV. 9. 1294^{a}11; *Rhet.* I. 8. 1366^{a}5). Champions of democracy regard it as a free society where one is able 'to live as one wishes' (VI. 2. 1317^{b}11–12; IV. 9. 1294^{a}11; *Rhet.* I. 8. 1366^{a}4). Advocates of aristocracy regard it as an ethical community directed to education and virtue (IV. 8. 1294^{a}9–11; *Rhet.* I. 8. 1366^{a}5–6). A contribution to one of these enterprises may not be a contribution to another. The very thing a joint-stock company pursues (profits) an ethical community may shun. Similarly, a quality (such as tightfistedness) that fits a man for a leadership position in a joint-stock company may not fit him for such a position in an ethical community. So in searching for the correct standard of worth Aristotle is led to the prime question: What is a political community? Or, in other words, what is a polis, or city?[17] The search for the correct conception of distributive justice becomes in the end a search for a definition of what it is to be a political community (see *Top.* VII. 3. 153^{a}15–16 and *Met.* VII. 5. 1031^{a}12).

6. What is a Political Community?

The definition of 'city' and the argument supporting it are found in chapter 9. Aristotle takes it for granted that a city is a kind of community (I. 1. 1252^{a}1, III. 3. 1276^{b}1). His argument boils down to a search for the feature that distinguishes a city from the other kinds within its genus. This feature, the differentia of a city, is its end, or goal. Aristotle attempts to can-

---

[17] For the question see III. 1. 1274^{b}32–4.

vass all the distinct possibilities, eliminating in turn all except one. He considers six possibilities:

1. Property (1280^a25–6)
2. Self-preservation (1280^a31)
3. Mutual defence against outsiders (1280^a34–5, $^b26$–7)
4. Trade and mutual intercourse (1280^a35–6)
5. Prevention of injustice to one another (1280^a39, $^b4$–5, 30–1)
6. Good life (1280^a31–2, $^b33$–5, 39)

Aristotle argues that taken severally or jointly the first five candidates differentiate at most an alliance, not a political community (1280^b8–33; see also II. 2. 1261^a24–5), and infers that the end of a city is good life (1280^b39). A city, he says, is 'a community of households and clans in living well, for the sake of a perfect and self-sufficient life' (1280^b33–5; see also VII. 8. 1328^a35–7). Combining this definition with the contribution-to-the task criterion, Aristotle concludes that 'those who contribute most to such a community have a larger share in the city than those who are equal or superior in freedom and birth but unequal in political virtue, or those who exceed in wealth but are exceeded in virtue' (1281^a4–8).

In saying that those possessing political virtue 'have a larger share in the city' than the free or the wealthy, Aristotle implies that the free and the wealthy also have a share, albeit a smaller one, and that the correct standard of worth, though heavily weighted in favour of virtue, includes freedom and wealth as well as virtue (see also III. 12. 1283^a9–22). When Aristotle condenses this into a formula, it becomes 'virtue fully furnished with external means' (IV. 2. 1289^a31–3; VII. 1. 1323^b41–1324^a1), his idea being that virtue without wealth is impotent.

Aristotle's argument is open to several objections. First of all, his list of the possible ends of a city is incomplete. An end he mentions elsewhere but fails to mention here is that pursued by Sparta: conquest and war (II. 9. 1271^{b}2–3; VII. 2. 1324^{b}5–9, 2. 1325^{a}3–4, 14. 1333^{b}12–14). Secondly, in eliminating the first five candidates he relies on a controversial premiss—namely, that a city is more than an alliance and hence must have a higher end than an alliance. Philosophers who adopt a minimalist view of a political community will think such a premiss begs the question. They argue that a city *is* simply a kind of alliance along with commercial and military alliances. Just as a military alliance is an alliance of cities, a city is an alliance of households. Aristotle mentions two such minimalists, Lycophron (III. 9. 1280^{b}10–12) and Hippodamus (II. 8; see especially 1267^{b}37–9). Finally, Aristotle's conclusion seems patently false. For good life is not an end that very many political communities pursue. Aristotle himself does not know of a single one. But one way to defeat a definition, as he points out, is to show that it is not true of every member of the species being defined: 'for the definition of "man" must be true of every man' (*Top.* VI. 1. 139^{a}25–7).

Aristotle has a reply to the last objection. His claim is not that his definition applies to every city but only that it will be acceptable to those who 'give thought to good government' (1280^{b}6) and 'inquire accurately' (1280^{b}28). The reason they will accept it presumably is that they are convinced by Aristotle's naturalism. This is the view that a political community is a natural entity like an animal or a man (I. 2. 1252^{b}30, 1253^{a}2, 25; IV. 4. 1291^{a}24–8; VII. 8. 1328^{a}21–5). Now a natural entity can be in either a natural or an unnatural condition. A man, for example, is in a natural condition when his soul rules his body but in an unnatural condition otherwise (I. 5. 1254^{a}34–^{b}9). The definition of a natural entity defines the entity in a natural condition. Thus, in spite of the fact that some horses are born blind, the possession of sight is part of the definition of 'horse'. By this line of reasoning the definition of 'city' can say that good life is the end, or goal, of a city even though there are many cities—all those with mistaken constitutions—for which this is false, since all such cities are in an unnatural condition (III. 17. 1287ᵇ39–41).

This reply raises another question: Why is it according to nature for a city to have a correct constitution and contrary to nature for it to have a mistaken constitution? The answer to this question is twofold. One reason that correct constitutions are according to nature is spelt out in Aristotle's description of the constitution of the best city in chapters 8 through 10 of Book VII and is beyond the scope of this essay. Briefly, Aristotle thinks the constitution of his best city is according to nature because it fosters the true end of human life and because its social and political structure reflects the natural hierarchy of human beings and the natural stages of life. One reason mistaken constitutions are contrary to nature is that they lack this structure.

A second reason comes directly from Aristotle's philosophy of nature, according to which what is forced and what is contrary to nature are the same (*Phys.* IV. 8. 215ᵃ1–4, V. 6. 230ᵃ29–30; *Cael.* I. 2. 300ᵃ23; *GA* V. 8. 788ᵇ27). In Aristotelian physics, for example, fire moves upwards towards its natural place by nature, but downwards only by force and contrary to nature (*GC* II. 6. 333ᵇ26–30). This identification of the forced and the unnatural is a feature, not only of inanimate nature, but of the entire natural world (*GA* II. 4. 739ᵃ4, III. 8. 777ᵃ18–19, V. 8. 788ᵇ27; *EE* II. 8. 1224ᵃ15–30; *Rhet* I. 11. 1370ᵃ9), and partially explains why mistaken constitutions are contrary to nature: they rest on force. The rulers under such a constitution seek only their own advantage and treat those outside the constitution, the second-class citizens, as slaves (IV. 11. 1295ᵇ19–23 together with III. 6. 1278ᵇ32–7). Since these outsiders are free men (III. 6. 1279ᵃ21; see also IV. 6. 1292ᵇ38–41), there can be no question of their enduring such treatment willingly (see IV. 10. 1295ª17–23). Thus, under a mistaken constitution there is always a group of subjects who obey their rulers only because they are forced to: the rich in a democracy, the poor in an oligarchy, the free in a tyranny (for tyranny see III. 14. 1285ª25–9, V. 11. 1314ª10–12).

Correct constitutions differ from mistaken constitutions in this respect and are according to nature, not only because of their structure, but also because they are free of the use of force. These two reasons are not unconnected. The best city of Book VII is free of force because its social and political structure is according to nature (see VII. 9. 1329ª2–17).

One can understand now why Aristotle's definition of 'the city truly so called' (III. 9. 1280ᵇ6–8), unlike the standard modern definition of the state,[18] makes no reference to compulsion or coercion. The use or threat of force is not in Aristotle's view an intrinsic part of a political community but an aberration like blindness in a horse.

An anomaly remains. For Aristotle holds that what is according to nature happens always or for the most part (*Phys.* II. 8. 198ᵇ35–6, *GC* II. 6. 333ᵇ4–7), whereas what is contrary to nature happens only rarely (*Phys.* II. 6. 197ᵇ34–5, 8. 198ᵇ36; *Met.* VI. 2. 1026ᵇ27–1027ª17). This is the reverse of what Aristotle found in the political realm. Most Greek cities in the fourth century were oligarchies or democracies. For a city to have a correct constitution and be in a natural condition was the exception, rather than the rule.[19]

7. The Many and the One

In chapter 13 Aristotle presents a puzzle facing all who dispute about political honours (1283ᵇ13–35). According to this

[18] *The Oxford Companion to Politics of the World* (Oxford, 1993), s.v. 'state'.

[19] Jonathan Lear in *Aristotle: The Desire to Understand* (Cambridge, 1988) thinks this anomaly reveals a tension between Aristotle, the 'teleological biologist', and Aristotle, the 'descriptive biologist' (p. 204).

puzzle any section of a city that makes a claim for political office on the basis of some particular standard of worth is open to a counterclaim from either the one or the many. Suppose the wealthy minority claim office on the basis of wealth. The richest man in the city can claim that by oligarchic justice he should rule alone. The many, on the other hand, can claim that they should rule since collectively they are richer than the few. Aristotle apparently accepts this line of reasoning. For he uses it in chapter 11 to give an Aristotelian justification of democracy and in chapter 13 to give an Aristotelian justification of absolute kingship. An Aristotelian justification is one that appeals to the conception of distributive justice that Aristotle regards as correct, the one that evaluates worth by the Aristotelian standard, 'virtue fully furnished with external means' (IV. 2. 1289^{a}31-3; VII. 1. 1323^{b}41-1324^{a}1).

In chapter 11 Aristotle claims that it sometimes happens that collectively the many are superior in virtue and practical wisdom to, and also richer than, the few best men. When this happens, Aristotle argues, the value of the offices allotted to the many should be greater than the value of the offices allotted to the few best men (1281^{a}40-^{b}21 together with 1282^{a}38-41; see also III. 13. 1283^{b}30-5). The idea behind this argument is that a group, deliberating together, may be wiser than its individual members taken separately (1281^{b}21-5). In general, a group may have an attribute that none of its members has (see II. 5. 1264^{b}20-1).

Aristotle uses a similar argument in chapter 13 to justify absolute kingship. In this chapter he is interested in the situation that arises when a man who is 'like a god among men' (1284^{a}10-11) appears in a political community. Such a man is incommensurably superior in virtue to everyone else both individually and collectively. Hence by the Aristotelian Principle the value of the offices allotted to him should be incommensurably superior to the value of the offices allotted to everyone else. Such a man should be made an absolute king who rules according to his own wish unrestricted by law (1284^a3–17, $^b25$–34; 16. 1287^a1–3, 8–10).[20] These two arguments turn on the little trick of applying the Aristotelian Principle to groups as well as individuals. Fully spelt out, the Aristotelian Principle asserts that if A and B are free adult males or groups of free adult males in a given city, then a distribution of political offices to A and B is just if, and only if, the value of the offices allotted to A stands to the value of the offices allotted to B as the virtue and wealth of A stands to the virtue and wealth of B. The two arguments have incompatible conclusions in spite of sharing the same major premiss. Democracy and absolute kingship cannot both be the right form of government for a given city at the same point in time. This does not mean that at least one of the arguments is invalid, but only that their unshared premisses are incompatible. In addition to the Aristotelian Principle, which the arguments share, each argument rests upon a minor premiss about the free adult males in a given city taken individually and collectively; and these minor premisses cannot both be true of the same city at the same time.

---

[20] There are a number of problems concerning Aristotle's theory of absolute kingship, including a question of internal consistency. It can be argued that on Aristotle's own principles absolute kingship does not deserve its premier ranking in his hierarchy of constitutions. For Aristotle appears to hold both that the moral development of the subjects of an absolute king will be stunted owing to their exclusion from political office and that the best constitution will promote the full moral development of the citizens who live under it. For a discussion of this question see Charles Kahn, 'The Normative Structure of Aristotle's "Politics" ', in Patzig, *Aristoteles' 'Politik'*, 380–1, and Miller, *Nature, Justice, and Rights*, 234–9.

8. *Paternalism*

We come finally to Aristotle's naturalism and alleged paternalism. Although Robinson treats these two topics together
(pp. xxii–xxvii), it may be better to separate them. The paternalist doctrine of the State, according to Robinson, is the
doctrine 'that the State is related to its citizens in the same
natural way as a father to his children, and ought to make and
keep its citizens virtuous as a father ought to make and keep
his children virtuous' (p. xi). Robinson thinks that Aristotle
subscribes to this doctrine and that it is 'the most fundamental and most grave error in Aristotle's politics' (p. xxii).

But there is reason to doubt that Aristotle would accept the
doctrine of paternalism as Robinson defines it. For he explicitly denies that political rule—rule among men who are free
and equal (I. 7. 1255^{b}20; III. 4. 1277^{b}7–13)—is the same as the
rule of a father over his children. Those who identify the two,
he claims, confuse political rule with the rule of a king (I. 12;
EE VII. 9. 1241^{b}29–31).

The doctrine of paternalism needs to be distinguished
from the view, of which Aristotle is a strong advocate, that the
citizens of a political community must be habituated and
educated in the spirit of its constitution if the community is
to survive (V. 9. 1310^{a}12–18). This view follows from two ideas,
that a political community can survive only if its laws are
obeyed, and that obedience to the law is a matter of habituation (II. 8. 1269^{a}20–1; *MA* 10. 703^{a}29–34). Aristotle notes that a
political community as well as an individual can suffer from
weakness of will, or *akrasia* (V. 9. 1310^{a}18–19). This happens
when a city has good laws but its laws are not obeyed (*EN* VII.
11. 1152^{a}19–23).

The sort of education and habituation that Aristotle envisages is primarily education and habituation in the moral
virtues, especially the cardinal virtues justice, bravery, and

temperance. Since justice is the glue that holds a political community together, it will need to be fostered under every constitution (except tyranny), though the sort of justice—democratic, oligarchic, and so forth—will vary from one to another. Bravery will be important in any city that has foreign enemies; and without temperance citizens are likely to be insolent to each other, which can lead to faction. Each of the cardinal virtues has a strong social rationale (VII. 15. 1334^{a}11–40), and the best city will cultivate them all.

The view that the citizens of a political community need a moral education is good social policy, not paternalism. Robinson admits as much when he acknowledges the importance of common decency among citizens (p. xxiv). Common decency is a complex virtue that awaits analysis. It is not obvious that it is a less exacting standard than the one Aristotle advocates. In any case common decency is a moral virtue the possession of which cannot be taken for granted, and the young people in a political community will not grow up possessing it if their elders do not teach it.

9. Naturalism

The naturalism of the *Politics* consists of two complementary theses, that the city is a natural entity (I. 2. 1252^{b}30, 1253^{a}2, 25; VII. 8. 1328^{a}21–5), and that man is by nature a political animal (I. 2. 1253^{a}2–3; III. 6. 1278^{b}19; *EN* I. 5. 1097^{b}11). As we saw in sections 5 and 6 above, the former thesis is the basis of Aristotle's theory of distributive justice. The Aristotelian conception of distributive justice, the true conception in Aristotle's view, combines the concept of distributive justice with what he takes to be the correct standard of worth. This standard is tied to Aristotle's definition of what it is to be a city, which describes the natural condition of a city. Since only a natural entity can be in a natural condition, the idea that the city is a natural entity is one of the main premisses of Aristotle's argument.

But not the only one. To reach a conclusion about justice Aristotle also needs a premiss connecting nature and goodness. The idea that a city is a natural entity can support Aristotle's theory of distributive justice only if the natural condition of a city is a good condition, only if what is natural is good. But Aristotle believes this; for he subscribes to a teleological view of nature according to which 'nature makes everything for the sake of something' (I. 2. 1252^{b}32; *PA* I. 1. 641^{b}12, 5. 645^{a}23–6; *Phys.* II. 8), where this something, the end, or goal, of the making, is something good (I. 1. 1252^{b}34–1253^{a}1; *Phys.* II. 2. 194^{a}32–3, 3. 195^{a}23–5; *Met.* I. 3. 983^{a}31–2).[21] Robinson explains why this view must be rejected (pp. xx, xxii–xxiii). The bedrock upon which Aristotle's theory comes to rest is also the rock upon which it founders.

It is the wreck of a noble project—to construct a theory of justice that avoids moral relativism without invoking a suprasensible realm of ethical and political ideals or a supernatural being. The greatness of the *Politics* resides precisely in its fully developed (though ultimately unsuccessful) response to the opposite challenges of Protagorean relativism and Platonism. Protagorean relativism is the view that 'whatever things *appear* just and fine to each city *are* so for it as long as it holds by them' (Plato, *Theat.* 167c4–5). According to this view, no conception of distributive justice is superior to any other; and, consequently, no city has an unjust constitution. Plato, like Aristotle, tries to avoid Protagorean relativism by an appeal to nature (*Laws* X. 888d7–890d8). But Plato's concept of nature is radically different from Aristotle's. Plato identifies the realm of nature with the world of Forms (see *Phdo.* 103b5; *Rep.* X. 597b5–7, c2, 598a1–3; and *Parm.* 132d2)

[21] In one passage, both points are combined: 'We say that nature makes for the sake of something, and that this is some good' (*Somn.* 2. 455^{b}17–18).

and finds his standard of justice in that world. He takes 'the just by nature' (*Rep.* VI. 501b2) to be the Form of justice, an incorporeal entity (*Phdo.* 65d4–66a10; *Soph.* 246b8) that exists beyond time and space (*Tim.* 37c6–38c3, 51c6–52b2). Aristotle wishes to avoid Protagorean relativism without invoking such a suprasensible standard. He identifies nature with the sensible world (*Met.* XII. 1. 1069^{a}30–^{b}2) and finds his standard of worth in this world. Aristotle's theory may run aground, but it does not sink under the weight of its ontology. [22]

[22] I am grateful to John Ackrill, Lindsay Judson, and my wife, Christine Keyt, for many helpful suggestions on earlier versions of this essay.

SELECT BIBLIOGRAPHY

Texts, translations, and commentaries

AUBONNET, JEAN, *Aristote, Politique*, text, French translation, and notes, 3 vols. (Budé; Paris, 1960–89).

BARKER, ERNEST, *The Politics of Aristotle*, translation with introduction, notes, and appendices (Oxford, 1946).

DREIZEHNTER, ALOIS, *Aristoteles' Politik*, text (Munich, 1970).

EVERSON, STEPHEN, *Aristotle, The Politics*, trans. Benjamin Jowett, rev. Jonathan Barnes (Cambridge, 1988).

IMMISCH, OTTO, *Aristotelis Politica*, text with scholia and glosses (Teubner; Leipzig, 1929).

LORD, CARNES, *Aristotle, The Politics*, translation with introduction, notes, and glossary (Chicago, 1984).

NEWMAN, W. L., *The Politics of Aristotle*, text, introduction, notes critical and explanatory, 4 vols. (Oxford, 1887–1902; repr. 1973).

RACKHAM, H., *Aristotle, Politics*, text and translation (Loeb Classical Library; Cambridge, Mass., 1932).

ROSS, W. D., *Aristotelis Politica* (Oxford Classical Texts; Oxford, 1957).

SCHÜTRUMPF, ECKART, *Aristoteles Politik*, vols. i and ii (Books I–III) (Berlin, 1991). Contains a full bibliography of works in both English and German.

SINCLAIR, T. A., *Aristotle, The Politics*, translation. 2nd rev. edn. by Trevor J. Saunders (Harmondsworth, 1983).

SUSEMIHL, FRANZ, and HICKS, R. D., *The Politics of Aristotle*, text, introduction, analysis, and commentary to Books I–V [I–III, VII–VIII] (London, 1894; repr. 1976).

Books

BARKER, ERNEST, *The Political Thought of Plato and Aristotle* (London, 1906; repr. 1959).

BARNES, JONATHAN, SCHOFIELD, MALCOLM, and SORABJI, RICHARD (eds.),

Articles on Aristotle 2: Ethics and Politics (London, 1977). Contains an annotated bibliography.

BIEN, GÜNTHER, *Die Grundlegung der politischen Philosophie bei Aristoteles* (Freiburg and Munich, 1973).

BODÉÜS, RICHARD, *The Political Dimensions of Aristotle's Ethics*, trans. Jan Edward Garrett (Albany, NY, 1993). Contains a full bibliography.

BRAUN, EGON, *Das dritte Buch der aristotelischen 'Politik': Interpretation* (Vienna, 1965).

DEFOURNY, MAURICE, *Aristote: Études sur la Politique* (Paris, 1932).

FOUNDATION HARDT, *Entretiens sur l'Antiquité Classique IX, La 'Politique' d'Aristote* (Geneva, 1964).

GALSTON, WILLIAM A., *Justice and the Human Good* (Chicago, 1980).

GLOTZ, GUSTAV, *La Cité grecque* (Paris, 1928).

HAVELOCK, E. A., *The Liberal Temper in Greek Politics* (New Haven and London, 1957), chs. 11–12.

HIGNETT, C., *A History of the Athenian Constitution to the End of the Fifth Century B.C.* (Oxford, 1952).

HOBBES, THOMAS, *Leviathan* (London, 1651).

IRWIN, TERENCE, *Aristotle's First Principles* (Oxford, 1988), chs. 16–22.

JAEGER, WERNER, *Aristotle: Fundamentals of the History of his Development*, trans. Richard Robinson, 2nd edn. (Oxford, 1948), ch. 10.

JOHNSON, CURTIS N., *Aristotle's Theory of the State* (London, 1990).

KAMP, ANDREAS, *Die politische Philosophie des Aristoteles und ihre metaphysischen Grundlagen* (Freiburg, 1985). Contains a bibliography of works in both English and German.

KEYT, DAVID, and MILLER, FRED D., JR. (eds.), *A Companion to Aristotle's Politics* (Oxford, 1991). Contains a full bibliography.

LEAR, JONATHAN, *Aristotle: The Desire to Understand* (Cambridge, 1988), ch. 5.

LEYDEN, W. VON, *Aristotle on Equality and Justice: His Political Argument* (London, 1985).

LORD, CARNES, *Education and Culture in the Political Thought of Aristotle* (Ithaca, NY, 1982).

—— and O'CONNOR, DAVID (eds.), *Essays on the Foundations of Aristotelian Political Science* (Berkeley, 1991).

MILLER, FRED D., JR., *Nature, Justice, and Rights in Aristotle's Politics* (Oxford, 1995). Contains a full bibliography.

MULGAN, R. G., *Aristotle's Political Theory* (Oxford, 1977).

NICHOLS, MARY P., *Citizens and Statemen: A Study of Aristotle's Politics* (Savage, Md., 1992).

PATZIG, GÜNTHER (ed.), *Aristoteles' 'Politik': Akten des XI. Symposium Aristotelicum* (Göttingen, 1990).

RAWLS, JOHN, *A Theory of Justice* (Cambridge, Mass., 1971).

ROSS, W. D., *Aristotle*, 5th edn. (London, 1949), ch. 8.

SABINE, GEORGE, *A History of Political Theory*, 4th edn. rev. Thomas Landon Thorson (Hinsdale, Ill., 1973), chs. 5–6.

SALKEVER, STEPHEN G., *Finding the Mean: Theory and Practice in Aristotelian Political Philosophy* (Princeton, 1990).

SCHÜTRUMPF, ECKART, *Die Analyse der Polis durch Aristotles*, 2 vols. (Amsterdam, 1980).

SINCLAIR, T. A., *A History of Greek Political Thought* (London, 1951), ch. 11.

STEINMETZ, PETER (ed.), *Schriften zu den Politika des Aristoteles* (Hildesheim, 1973).

SWANSON, JUDITH A., *The Public and the Private in Aristotle's Political Philosophy* (Ithaca, NY, 1992).

WOOD, ELLEN MEIKSINS, and WOOD, NEAL, *Class Ideology and Ancient Political Theory* (Oxford, 1978), ch. 5.

YACK, BERNARD, *The Problems of a Political Animal: Community, Justice, and Conflict in Aristotelian Political Thought* (Berkeley, 1993).

Articles

BARKER, ERNEST, 'The Life of Aristotle and the Composition and Structure of the Politics', *Classical Review*, 45 (1931), 162–72.

BOAS, GEORGE, 'A Basic Conflict in Aristotle's Philosophy', *American Journal of Philology*, 64 (1943), 172–93.

BRADLEY, A. C., 'Aristotle's Conception of the State', in Keyt and Miller, *Companion*, 13–56.

BRAUN, EGON, 'Die Summierungstheorie des Aristoteles', in Steinmetz, *Schriften*, 396–423.

COOPER, JOHN M., 'Political Animals and Civic Friendship', in Patzig, *Aristoteles' 'Politik'*, 220–41.

FORTENBAUGH, WILLIAM W., 'Aristotle on Prior and Posterior, Correct and Mistaken Constitutions', in Keyt and Miller, *Companion*, 226–37.

IRWIN, TERENCE, 'The Good of Political Activity', in Patzig, *Aristoteles' 'Politik'*, 73–100.

JOHNSON, CURTIS N., 'Who is Aristotle's Citizen?', *Phronesis*, 29 (1984), 73–90.

KAHN, CHARLES H., 'The Normative Structure of Aristotle's "Politics"', in Patzig, *Aristoteles' 'Politik'*, 369–84.

KEYT, DAVID, 'Aristotle and Anarchism', *Reason Papers*, no. 18 (Fall, 1993), 133–52.

—— 'Aristotle's Theory of Distributive Justice', in Keyt and Miller, *Companion*, 238–78.

—— 'Three Basic Theorems in Aristotle's *Politics*', in Keyt and Miller, *Companion*, 118–41.

MULGAN, R. G., 'A Note on Aristotle's Absolute Ruler', *Phronesis*, 19 (1974), 66–9.

—— 'Aristotle and Absolute Rule', *Antichthon*, 8 (1974), 21–8.

NEWMAN, W. L., 'Aristotle's Classification of Forms of Government', *Classical Review*, 6 (1892), 289–93.

ROWE, CHRISTOPHER, 'Aims and Methods in Aristotle's *Politics*', in Keyt and Miller, *Companion*, 57–74.

SIDGWICK, HENRY, 'Aristotle's Classification of Forms of Government', *Classical Review*, 6 (1892), 141–4.

STOCKS, J. L., 'The Composition of Aristotle's Politics', *Classical Quarterly*, 21 (1927), 177–87.

VANDER WAERDT, P. A., 'Kingship and Philosophy in Aristotle's Best Regime', *Phronesis*, 30 (1985), 249–73.

INDEX

Made in the USA
San Bernardino, CA
29 August 2018